CAN'T BEAT 'EM, EAT 'EM!

FEATURING
40 INVASIVE SPECIES
WITH RECIPES

by Chef Philippe Parola

Invasive Species Cause $120 Billion Annually in Environmental Damage
Saving the Ecosystem ONE BITE AT A TIME

Editor/Designer
Cody Sibley. Mystic Spiral Consulting

Copy Writer/Assistant Editor
Kristie F. Gauthreaux, Mask-Off Publishing

Copy Editor/Design Consultant
Sadie Roberts, Mystic Spiral Consulting

CAN'T BEAT 'EM, EAT 'EM!

FEATURING
40 INVASIVE SPECIES WITH RECIPES

by Chef Philippe Parola

ISBN 979-8-218-11653-8
Independently Published
Printed in the U.S.A.

Can't Beat 'Em, Eat 'Em, LLC
P.O. Box 84524
Baton Rouge, LA 70884

www.cantbeatemeatem.us

Copyright © 2023 Chef Philippe Parola. All Rights Reserved.
No portion of this book may be reproduced in any form without written permission of the copyright holder.

TABLE OF CONTENTS

Preface 2

Photo: Chef Philippe Parola 2

About the Author 3

Special Thank Yous 6
    Dedication 8
    Introduction 9

Tackling Invasive and Nuisance Species 10
    America, We Have A Problem: Invasive Species 10
    Alligator: From the Bayou to America's Menus 12
    Nutria: On the Grill 14
    From Invasive Carp to Delicious Copi 16
        How It All Began 16
        The Next Steps 17
        For the Skeptics 18
        Future Impact 18
    Why Eat Invasive Carp? Roy Brabham, M.D. 19
    The Mississippi River Basin: 1.5 Million Miles of River 20
    "Well, Chef, They Sure Jumped in the Wrong Boat" 21
    Invasive Carp Recipe Places 3rd In NOLA Navy Cook-Off 22
    Invasive Silver Carp Navy Cook-Off Recipe 23
    A Crawfish Tale: From Mud Bugs to Multi-Millions 24
    Gen-Z Eager to Make a Difference (Photo Collage) 26
    Louisiana and Illinois Find [Invasive] Carp Solution by Ewell Smith 27
    As Chef Philippe Always Says: Can't Beat 'Em, Eat 'Em! 30

Invasive FISH Species with Recipes 33
    Profile: Silver Carp aka Copi 34
    Recipe: Copi (Silver Carp) Fish Cakes 35
    Profile: Brown Trout 36
    Recipe: Brown Trout Pecan 37
    Profile: Black Carp aka Copi 38
    Recipe: Cajun Style Copi (Black Carp) 39
    Profile: Lionfish 40
    Recipe: Lionfish Meunière 41
    Profile: Armored Sailfin Catfish 42
    Recipe: Armored Catfish in Wine and Capers 43
    Profile: Tilapia 44
    Recipe: Southern Baked Tilapia 45
    Profile: Northern Snakehead Fish 46
    Recipe: Snakehead Fish Almondine 47
    Profile: Grass Carp aka Copi 48
    Recipe: Copi (Grass Carp) Au Gratin 49
    Profile: Swamp Eel 50
    Recipe: Swamp Eel Stir Fry 51
    Profile: Bighead Carp aka Copi 52

TABLE OF CONTENTS

    Recipe: Copi (Bighead Carp) Sliders 53
    Notes Sheet 54

Invasive SHELLFISH Species with Recipes 55
    Profile: Red Crawfish 56
    Recipe: Cajun Style Boiled Red Crawfish 57
    Profile: European Green Crab 58
    Recipe: Green Crab Bisque 59
    Profile: Black Tiger Shrimp 60
    Recipe: Shrimp in Lemon Cream Sauce 61
    Profile: Golden Clam 62
    Recipe: Golden Clam Chowder 63
    Profile: Zebra Mussel 64
    Recipe: Stuffed Zebra Mussel 65
    Profile: Apple Snail 66
    Recipe: Apple Snail Provençale 67
    Notes Sheet 68

Invasive MAMMAL Species with Recipes 69
    Profile: Feral Swine (Wild Boar) 70
    Recipe: Sweet Berry Wild Boar 71
    Profile: Fox Squirrel 72
    Recipe: Fox Squirrel Ravigote 73
    Profile: Nutria 74
    Recipe: Ragondin (Nutria) Crock Pot (Heart Healthy) 75
    Profile: European Rabbit 76
    Recipe: European Rabbit with Mushrooms 77
    Profile: Axis (Spotted Deer) 78
    Recipe: Axis Deer with Cherry Sauce 79
    Profile: Feral Goat 80
    Recipe: Feral Goat Dijon 81
    Notes Sheet 82

Invasive AVIAN Species with Recipes 83
    Profile: Muscovy Duck 84
    Recipe: Muscovy Duck à L'Orange 85
    Profile: Rock Dove (Common Pigeon) 86
    Recipe: Rock Dove (Pigeon) Stew 87
    Profile: Snow Goose 88
    Recipe: One Pot Glazed Snow Goose 89
    Profile: Canada Goose 90
    Recipe: Canada Goose Parmigiana 91
    Notes Sheet 92

Invasive REPTILE and AMPHIBIAN Species with Recipes 93
    Profile: Green Iguana 94
    Recipe: Fried Green Iguana Tacos 95

TABLE OF CONTENTS

Profile: Burmese Python 96
Recipe: Gourmet Python Burgers 97
Profile: Red-Eared Slider Turtle 98
Recipe: Red-Eared Slider Turtle Soup 99
Profile: American Bullfrog 100
Recipe: Fried Bullfrog Legs 101
Notes Sheet 102

Invasive PLANT Species with Recipes 103
Profile: Kudzu Vine 104
Recipe: Kudzu Pie 105
Profile: Himalayan Blackberry 106
Recipe: Himalayan Blackberry Flambé 107
Profile: Autumn Olive/Berry 108
Recipe: Autumn Olive Jelly 109
Profile: Garlic Mustard 110
Recipe: Garlic Mustard Pasta 111
Profile: Wintercress 112
Recipe: Creamy Wintercress Dip 113
Profile: Purslane 114
Recipe: Purslane Salad 115
Profile: Japanese Knotweed 116
Recipe: Knotweed Garlic Butter 117
Profile: Strawberry Guava 118
Recipe: Strawberry Guava Toast 119
Profile: Dandelion 120
Recipe: Dandelion Bacon Vinaigrette Salad 121
Profile: European Water Chestnut 122
Recipe: Candied European Water Chestnuts 123
Notes Sheet 124

BONUS INVASIVE SPECIES RECIPES 125
Bonus Recipe: Can't Beat 'Em, Eat 'Em INVASALAYA™ 126
Bonus Recipe: Can't Beat 'Em, Eat 'Em GUMBO 127
Notes Sheet 128

Supportive Statements and Letters from Experts 129
What the Experts Say 130
A Letter from Chef Michael Johnson 132
Support from Louisiana Seafood Exchange 133
Support from Tim Ruth at Louisiana Wildlife and Fisheries 134
Can't Beat 'Em, Eat 'Em Cartoon 136

INDEX 137

INVASIVE SPECIES AND RECIPE QUICK REFERENCE 141

CHEF PHILIPPE PAROLA

ABOUT THE AUTHOR

French Chef Philippe Parola, "Commandeur des Cordon Bleu de France", grew up in the 1960s in Chalouze, a tiny village near the beautiful town of Ebreuil in central France. He is an orphan raised in a foster family by Louis and Clotilde Lapendrie. In those years, hunting, trapping, and fishing were the most efficient and economical ways to produce food on the table, a skill set he developed early in life.

A 1975 graduate of Culinary Art - Charcuterie, Chef Philippe migrated to New Orleans in the early 1980s to work at a famous Louisiana restaurant. His love for sport-fishing, hunting, and the great outdoors made it easy to transition into the Louisiana lifestyle, a state known as the Sportsman's Paradise. His boyhood experiences in the outdoors and the Louisiana lifestyle paved the way for international recognition of Chef Philippe's exotic, innovative cuisine.

His recipes have been featured in hundreds of local, national, and international media stories, with most notable appearances on NBC, NPR, ESPN, CNN, ABC World News, Vice News, CBS, France 2, South Korean TV, Japan's Kyodo News, Taiwan News, China Post, Modern Farmer, PBS, Animal Planet, National Geographic, Smithsonian, Hemisphere Magazine, Field and

Prestigious Cordon Bleu Medallion Award

Chef Philippe Parola serving the 41st President of the United States, George H. W. Bush.

Chef Philippe Parola serving the 38th President of the United States, Gerald R. Ford.

"This was one of my most memorable experiences as a professional chef. Both presidents were extraordinarily amiable." - Chef Philippe

Stream Magazine, The New York Times, The Atlantic, Jeremy Wade's Mighty Rivers series, and Jeff Corwin's Extreme Cuisines on the Food Network.

In the 1980s and 1990s, Chef Philippe received the Silver Plate National Award from the Chaine des Rotisseur and the Presidential Medallion when he cooked for the United States Presidents Alumni Dinner. He also earned the title of Commandeur de la Commanderie des Cordon Bleu de France, membership in Les Toques Blanches International, the All-Japan Chef's Association, and the All-Canadian Chef's Association. He also represented the United States at the International Food Expo (SIAL) in Paris & Frankfurt, Germany, and Tokyo (FoodEx).

Starting as an orphan born and raised in a tiny village in central France, Chef eventually moved to the United States to the French Cajun country of Louisiana. Nowhere else could an orphan boy raised by foster parents, emigrate to a foreign land, and be given the opportunity and honor to serve not one, but two, U.S. Presidents. France gave him his education, and the U.S. gave him opportunities.

Chef Philippe worked at several prestigious Louisiana restaurants and owned a fine-dining French restaurant. In those capacities, he welcomed and trained young people as his apprentices. Later, Chef Philippe opened and operated a culinary school to educate even more young chefs.

Among his apprentices were Chef Tim Creehan, owner, and celebrity chef at the nationally acclaimed Cuvee 30A, on the Florida Emerald Coast, and Michael Johnson, now the Executive Chef at the athletic department of Louisiana State University, where he is responsible for the diets for world-class athletes.

Over the years, as his career progressed, national and international recognition for his innovative cuisine came. At the peak of his restaurant career came the 2003 French backlash, where some politicians started calling French fries "Freedom Fries."

This was a dark period for him which forced Chef Philippe out of the restaurant industry. It was a turning point where he realized it was essential to turn the negative into a positive.

Young 24-year-old Chef Philippe (r) pictured with his 16-year-old, first apprentice, and now celebrity Chef Tim Creehan, the proud owner of Cuvee 30A on Florida's Emerald Coast.

Therefore, he focused more on the research and development toward the edibility of invasive species that could save the ecosystem.

Consequently, cooking wild game and exotic animal meat became his specialty. Over the years, he's prepared dishes with hundreds of species. It is often said of the people of Louisiana that they will eat anything. Naturally, his experiences and recipe successes eventually led him to consider invasive species as a potential food source and a means of diminishing their population. ✠

U. S. Ambassador to Japan Tom Foley (c), Tim Creehan (r) with me in Tokyo representing the USA at Foodex International Food Exhibit.

SPECIAL THANK YOUS

David Roshto cooking Invasalaya™ at Fred's On the River in Prairieville, Louisiana.

Chef Philippe's foster sister Sylvie (l), and his two daughters visiting his foster mom Clotilde (r) in the tiny French village Chalouze where he learned how to fish and hunt.

David Roshto

David Roshto has been my close friend for 40 years. We love recreational fishing, hunting, and other outdoor activities. We've conjured up multiple ways to cook the invasive species talked about in this book and other wild games. We've tested the recipes by cooking together in Fred's On the River kitchen in Prairieville, Louisiana. Without David's assistance, this book would not be a reality. ✠

My Family in France

My upbringing in rural central France gave me a lasting appreciation for nature. Clotilde and Louis Lapendrie, raised a large family, two girls, Sylvie and Alice, three boys, Serge, Gilles, and me. Louis taught me to hunt and fish. I will always remember him saying, "You kill it, you eat it." Clotilde taught me to cook at an early age. As Clotilde approaches her 100th birthday, it makes me believe that eating what nature provides is the secret to a long, healthy life. My biological sister Patricia, an excellent cook and supportive of a clean environment, was adopted but found me here in the United States when I was 30. I have become very close with Patricia and her husband, Anton. ✠

Patricia, Chef Philippe's sister, and her husband Anton enjoying a sweet treat.

Cody Sibley
Mystic Spiral Consulting

Kristie F. Gauthreaux
Mask-Off Publishing

Aurbin Dickey

Chef Philippe's surrogate father and champion Domino player, Aurbin Dickey, is a food connoisseur who loves wild-caught fish and supports wildlife preservation.

A special thank you is due to my friend Cody Sibley for his never ending support. His experience and expertise were a true asset as the Editor and Graphic Designer for this book. I must also recognize Kristie F. Gauthreaux, our Copy Editor and Editorial Assistant, with Mask-Off Publishing. Her collaboration with the rest of the team to bring this book from idea to publication has been invaluable.

Deepest gratitude also goes to Bill and Alla Baltas of Alla's Fine Art in Baton Rouge, Louisiana for restoration of old photos. Such gratitude also goes to Vasken Kaltakdjian and Sami Kobrossi with Serop's restaurants in Baton Rouge, Louisiana and Chef Cullen Lord of Real Cajun Market in Fayette County, Georgia for all of their support through the years..

There have been literally hundreds of men and women that have been supportive of my idea to help control invasive species by utilizing them as a food source. It would take pages to name them all, and undoubtedly, I would forget someone. So, I won't attempt to list them. But they know who they are and to each of you, accept my gratitude and this acknowledgment.

Most importantly, I must acknowledge my family for all of their love and support.

Chef Philippe's close friends supporting Can't Beat 'Em Eat 'Em's quest to preserve wildlife habitat for future generations. Linda Bynum, first left the late John Graves, second left, and his wife Cynthia Graves, third left, parents of Louisiana Congressman Garret Graves, a huge Louisiana outdoor enthusiast who supports preserving wildlife habitat. On my far right, former Louisiana Natural Resources Secretary John Ales, illustrious restaurateur Gino Marino (Gino's Restaurant, Baton Rouge), second right, and my dear friend and big brother-like, Glen Bynum, (third right).

DEDICATION

Chef Philippe Parola with his inspirations: his daughters Danielle (immediate left) and Jolie (right), and family member Ariana (far left).

"My passion for writing this book and seeing it published is born of love for your children and my children."

Chef Philippe Parola with his partner in life, Alaine

This book is dedicated to my daughters, Danielle and Jolie, and my partner in life, Alaine Knight (Jolie's mother). My passion for writing this book and seeing it published is born of love for your children and my children. It is my greatest desire for us to leave them a legacy that we made a difference in preserving the fragile ecosystems of our state, our nation, and our world.

My solution to the invasive species, Can't Beat 'Em, Eat 'Em might not be proven soon. But with the world's population, today exceeding 8 billion people and the present and future forecasts in food supply versus demand and ongoing higher prices, which made food less affordable to many. It's safe to say that in 10 to 20 years, my theory will be in the works! This concept is critical for your children, my children, and future generations. Today, I challenge you to reconsider your food choices and beliefs about what you eat and waste.

"This concept is critical for your children, my children, and future generations."

INTRODUCTION

Here are my daughters; when they were younger, enjoying fishing. Let's preserve our outdoors so our future generations can enjoy it!

"It is imperative that we leave a legacy to preserve the joy of outdoor activities for future generations. We must be proactive and better stewards! This solution will prevent us from being so wasteful when hunger and poverty is a growing domestic and international crisis."

Chef Philippe

The late Cajun humorist and television cook Justin Wilson once asked the rhetorical question. "Who was the hungriest man that ever lived? The first man to eat a raw oyster! Indeed, whoever picked up a bi-valve mollusk curious enough to open it, no easy task to see if there was something edible inside, must have been extraordinarily hungry.

People have eaten wild game and harvested plants for food since early man. Practically all that we eat would not be food had it not first been harvested from the wild. Today, many people hunt, trap, harvest, and fish to provide food for their families.

This book is more than a cookbook. It is meant to educate you about invasive species, which can do irreparable harm to our ecosystem. Toward the end of the book, you will find supportive letters from several wildlife experts.

I encourage you to cook and eat invasive species as a natural source of proteins, vitamins, and minerals. You can easily adapt the gourmet-minded recipes featured in this book to your regional flair.

Eating invasive species will also encourage commercial harvesting of these species to protect the environment and provide a sustainable food source to feed a hungry world. My solution, Can't Beat 'Em Eat 'Em, will create many new jobs where they are needed the most and boost local economies.

While the included species are healthy to eat, to prevent bacterial cross-contamination, please wash all invasive species thoroughly and cook them until well done.

Many plants, mollusks, crustaceans, reptiles, birds, and mammals are found in the woods, rivers, lakes, or ponds near you. There are many authorities at different levels of government involved. Usually, the state Wildlife and Fisheries agencies make the final determination regarding whether a species is considered invasive.

States also work closely with federal agencies. Always consult your state government about state and federal rules or laws about hunting, trapping, harvesting, or fishing invasive species.

Tackling Invasive and Nuisance Species

AMERICA, WE HAVE A PROBLEM: INVASIVE SPECIES

Successful Wild Boar hunt in Venice, Louisiana. This wild beast fed over 200 people!

America, we have a problem! It costs you billions, and you probably don't even know about it. I'm Chef Philippe Parola, and my solution is simple and transparent if we Can't Beat 'Em, Eat 'Em.

Non-native species (plants and animals) that cause economic, environmental, or human-health harm are considered invasive species. It is often incredibly detrimental when non-native species invade the ecosystems of indigenous or native species.

Invasive species are the leading cause of the decline in native wildlife populations. In some cases, native species have been nearly reduced to extinction. In other words, invasive species can lead to extinction.

Studies indicate that invasive species annually cause over $120 billion in damage in the USA. That includes environmental destruction, reduced agricultural productivity, decreased property values, the strain on public utility operations, diminished freshwater quality, and commercial fisheries interference.

These invaders also negatively impact recreational hunting and fishing. Perhaps most importantly, they disrupt the overall health of the ecosystem! And that is without considering the detrimental impact around the world.

Just to reiterate: 120 billion US Dollars per year in damage caused by invasive species. Then there are millions of dollars spent annually on feasibility studies to find short and long-term methods to eradicate these species. Experience indicates that research toward the eradication of invasive species has proved ineffective because it is very difficult to achieve.

Despite the inquiries, efforts, and dollars thrown at the problem, time has demonstrated that complete eradication of invasive species is impossible without a greater negative impact on native species and the ecosystem. In other words, we are spending billions of dollars trying to eradicate species that are, in many cases, perfectly natural food sources.

Because of it, future generations may judge our time as ineffective in this battle. I want my kids, yours, and future generations to enjoy the

Tackling Invasive and Nuisance Species

outdoors as much as I did. So, my challenge is, let's make a difference to preserve natural wildlife habitats for future generations!

What if there is another way to prevent costly destruction from invasive species? There could be a national research center with a test kitchen to create recipes and sanitation protocols to prevent bacteria cross-contamination for food production utilizing invasive plant and animal species. Or, what about research extracting vitamins, minerals, and other substances that would benefit humanity? What about starting to eat invasive species?

Educating people on how to safely and tastefully cook invasive species could increase the harvest of these species easily found in nearby woods, fields, ponds, lakes, and rivers. Together we can impact their populations ONE BITE AT A TIME to the point that invasive species are able to co-exist with native species without harming the ecosystem. Yes, we can do it!

There is growing hunger around the world. The U. S. Department of Housing says the growth in homelessness has increased significantly since the pandemic's start. Homelessness translates to hunger.

There is no better time to start reducing invasive species populations and rebuilding wildlife habitats. From wild boar to Invasive carp, Kudzu vine to Burmese Python, Zebra Mussels, and others, I say,

Can't Beat 'Em, Eat 'Em!

Chef Philippe is hands-on in research and development for invasive species recipes.

Chef Philippe says, "I enjoyed a field trip, sharing my knowledge with young people in Illinois about preserving ecosystems from invasive species."

TACKLING INVASIVE AND NUISANCE SPECIES

ALLIGATOR: FROM THE BAYOU TO AMERICA'S MENUS

In the 1950s, years of unregulated harvesting impacted the alligator population. By 1962 the Louisiana Department of Wildlife and Fisheries halted alligator harvesting altogether.

The plan was to restore the alligator population, which had diminished to under 100,000 and it was listed as an endangered species. In one of the greatest success stories in wildlife and ecological management, by 1972, the alligator population had increased to the point that it required a small, managed, sustainable harvest.

The alligator was removed from the "endangered" list two years later. Today there are over 2 million alligators in Louisiana in natural habitats and another 1 million on managed farms.

A decade before my arrival, In the 1970s, Egon Klein migrated to Louisiana. He had come to Louisiana, where he built a successful business exporting alligator hides to Europe to be tanned for use as handbags, shoes, and accessories.

When the animal rights movement began to build in Europe, demand for animal skins and furs plummeted. Egon's export business suffered a significant downturn.

A true entrepreneur and the most charismatic individual I ever knew, Egon was also European. A Romanian, Egon spent much

It was the early 1980s --- So young and naive. Even cooking alligator meat didn't scare me! Sous Chef Kent Fontenot (l), Me (c), Apprentice Chef Lance Houston (r), David Hunter, Dining Manager (fr)

Tackling Invasive and Nuisance Species

of his childhood in a Nazi Concentration Camp in World War II. The tattoo on his wrist constantly reminded me of what he had endured. When his business faced the potential of failure, he asked if I could create recipes using alligator meat. If I could, then it might save his business. Wild game was one thing; the alligator, exotic animal meat was another.

But, by the 1980s, the alligator population exploded to the point of being a nuisance. Managing their population without a commercial market for hides meant killing animals purely for population control. Yet in those days, even when the alligator hide was used, I realized the alligator meat had gone to waste. That made me angry.

After I accepted Egon's challenge, the recipes came together, and off I went with alligator recipes promoting it as a delicacy. One can only imagine how inefficient that was before cell phones and the internet. It was a challenging sale as well.

Still, the result was that alligator meat is now a multi-million-dollar business growing in Louisiana and Florida, and other states.

Louisiana is home to many "invasive" species partly because of the state's subtropical climate and almost countless waterways. That includes the Mississippi Basin Delta, where fresh water meets salt water, creating a unique wildlife harmony.

Unfortunately, this unique wildlife habitat is in imminent danger from several invasive species, including the Nutria, Wild Boar, and the notorious destructive invasive carp.

TACKLING INVASIVE AND NUISANCE SPECIES

NUTRIA: ON THE GRILL

The experience I had with alligator meat exposed me to the professionals at Louisiana Wildlife and Fisheries. The growing success of marketing gator meat brought those professionals to me in search of a similar solution.

Unlike the native alligator, which was an integral part of the ecosystem, the Nutria was an invasive species in the state of Louisiana.

Demand for nutria fur, primarily in the Soviet Union, where these were valued in hat making for their cold winters, diminished with the collapse of the Soviet Government. The dissolution of the Soviet Government led to an economic downturn in the region that dropped prices for nutria fur so low that trapping was no longer economically feasible.

The very prolific Nutria (Ragondin) endangered the ecosystem by devouring vegetation which accelerates coastal wetland erosion. The Louisiana Department of Wildlife and Fisheries challenged me to promote nutria meat.

In the 1990s, at the behest of the Louisiana Department

Chef says, "I was challenging myself with a whole Nutria. These cousins of the beaver are too often compared to another rodent, the rat. That scares people away from eating it. Nutria are strictly vegetarian in contrast to the rat. They feed on the stems and roots of plants, making the meat high in natural protein. It is the most nutritious red meat for human consumption."

of Wildlife and Fisheries, with the cooperation of the Louisiana Department of Agriculture, which granted the guidelines to process Nutria meat into food for human consumption.

The process was to have trappers catch and kill Nutria in the wild and, within the same day, transport the Nutria in a refrigerated truck to the state-inspected processing plant to process the Nutria meat. Those guidelines were also approved by the US, Food and Drug Administration (FDA) protocols to authorize eating Nutria meat within the state.

Tackling Invasive and Nuisance Species

Motivated, like me, to preserve our state's wetlands, several well-known Louisiana chefs rallied behind my marketing slogan, Can't Beat 'Em, Eat 'Em! The meat appeared on many restaurant menus and grocery stores in the form of sausages, stews, and gumbos.

This solution helped to incentivize trappers for commercial harvests. But a significant obstacle to its success arose when the Food and Drug Administration FDA prevented shipping the meat across state lines. The lack of that approval quelled a massive contract with the government of Taiwan.

The FDA responded that Nutria must be slaughtered live in front of the FDA inspectors before being processed for human consumption and shipped out across the Louisiana state line. That task was impossible to achieve at that time. I was confused and thought that one FDA branch approved our State guidelines for processing and eating Nutria meat in Louisiana, but another FDA branch condemned the interstate sales. Does that mean it is safe for us to eat Nutria meat in Louisiana but not good enough for the rest of the world?

At that juncture, the Louisiana Department of Wildlife and Fisheries withdrew its support from the effort. Instead, new protocols were issued, and trappers were financially incentivized to kill Nutria and cut off their tails to prove the kill. Often today, carcasses are left behind, regardless of how excellent the lean meat is for food protein. Nevertheless, many more people are eating nutria meat today primarily because of the effort made in the 1990s. Additionally, there is still interest from around the U.S. food markets places to purchase Nutria meat.

Many wildlife policymakers are cautioning you not to eat wild game due to the high risk of bacterial cross-contamination. Ironically, according to research, there are more than 3000 deaths in our country each year from eating conventional processed food. But no study to date has identified any potential deaths from the consumption of wild game.

NUTRIA NUTRITION				
NUTRITION	NUTRIA	CHICKEN	BEEF	TURKEY
Protein G/1000	22.1	21.4	16.6	21.8
Fat G/1000	1.5	3.1	26.6	2.9
Carb. G/1000	0	0	0	0
Cholesterol G/1000	40.1	70	85	65

Pan Fried Nutria with Noodles

Introducing nutria gumbo in New Orleans

Tackling Invasive and Nuisance Species

FROM INVASIVE CARP TO DELICIOUS *COPI*

The easily frightened invasive carp jump high out of the water. At 20 pounds and much larger, these jumping fish land in boats and have a high potential to cause injury or even death to fishermen and water sports enthusiasts. Photo: Thad Cook, Illinois Department of Natural Resources.

❦ How It All Began ❧

In the summer of 2009, the Food Network invited me to participate in an Extreme Cuisine episode with Jeff Corwin. The segment was to feature cooking an Alligator Gar. Until the 1980s, these frightening-looking fish with sharp teeth were considered trash fish by most, detrimental to sports fishing.

Gar has historically been eaten by many in Louisiana and is now a delicacy. Later however, gar was recognized as an essential aspect of the ecology in their habitats. Unsurprisingly, Louisiana is part of the Alligator Gar's home range and is one of the few predators that prey on invasive carp.

Gladly accepting the opportunity, I called my friend, Billy Frioux, to catch the beastly fish. As we crossed the Atchafalaya River, giant fish began jumping out of the water. Several landed in our boat. In my years of cooking, I'd seen many fish species, but none looked like these. I asked Billy if he knew what fish these were. To my surprise, he replied, those are invasive carp.

I knew the invasive carp was creating a major concern in the Great Lakes area, and expensive efforts were started to block their entry into the Great Lakes. But I had no idea they had invaded Louisiana's waterways.

Looking at a couple of large carp in the boat, there were two choices: (1) throw them

TACKLING INVASIVE AND NUISANCE SPECIES

Louisiana fisherman Richard Verret and his two sons with a load of commercially harvested invasive carp.

back or (2) seize the opportunity to explore a food avenue for human consumption. One thing was sure as the thoughts ran through my head, human consumption and demand would lead to commercial fishing that could reduce the carp population and reduce their threat to native aquatic life. It may not surprise you that I wanted to cook it.

My thinking was clear. A solution to this invasive species would create jobs and boost local economies. Commercially processing this invasive species for human consumption would be the right thing to do.

☙ The Next Steps ❧

It took almost ten years to get from that fishing trip idea to the point of processing that single invasive species. Just the word "carp" created a significant barrier. Carp, with its complex bone structure, was the foremost negative. The connotation of the term invasive species made it worse. No one thought that my idea would work. Finally, that forced me to contract with a third party.

I received the help of the US Embassy in Vietnam, which I found to be a beautiful country with wonderful people. We sent fish there to be processed into fish cakes for food marketplaces in America. Several trips between Louisiana and Vietnam were required to train the locals with my recipes and protocols.

Finally, in 2019, I successfully marketed the new invasive carp product under my new brand, Silverfin . Name changes of several fish species, such as Patagonian toothfish, renamed Chilean Sea Bass, help to gain acceptance as a food item.

Invasive carp in the native range, Asia, are harvested as major aquaculture species for local human consumption. The hurdle is to get Americans to accept and appreciate these species as a healthy food source.

The COVID-19 pandemic in March 2020 stopped import/export from Vietnam and discontinued product distribution in the US. With the negative always comes a positive. With a group of close friends, we are working to establish protocols for a new processing plant in the United States for several value-added fish products for human consumption. We hope to have several new **COPI** fish products caught and processed in the USA in the near future.

Chef Philippe Parola greets President Truong Tan Sang of the Republic of Vietnam.

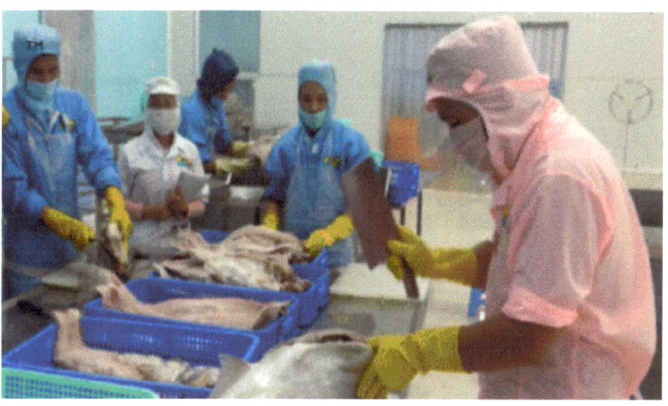

Invasive carp processing into fish cakes in Vietnam.

Tackling Invasive and Nuisance Species

⋘ For the Skeptics ⋙

This is for skeptics that don't believe in our proposed invasive species solution.

In the 1980s, my dear friend, and American culinary legend, the late Chef Paul Prudhomme introduced "Blackened Redfish" as a delicacy. The popularity of just that one recipe led to overfishing Redfish species on the Gulf coast to the point that to protect redfish populations, governments in the states bordering the gulf placed significant limitations on the numbers caught. So, changing dietary habits, leading to harvesting food, can impact the control of invasive species.

It takes a small leap to conclude that we can change the paradigm about eating an invasive plant or animal species. Or that in doing it, we can solve a significant challenge for the ecosystem while also providing nutritious meals to the peoples of the world.

⋘ Future Impact ⋙

Cooperation and coordination are required because invasive carp threaten the Mississippi River Basin's entire 1.5 million river miles. Illinois Department of Natural Resources successfully introduced the collective name **COPI** for each of the four species of invasive carp.

In my fourth decade of introducing invasive plant and animal species into the world's cuisine, my quest to solve a significant ecosystem issue goes forward. My vision is that our environment will be protected, man's stewardship of natural resources will improve, and people will shift their beliefs about food sources to improve nutrition and help end hunger.

Achieving my vision might take ten or twenty, even thirty or forty years from now, long after I'm gone. But what a legacy to leave for the generations yet to come to say no to being the most wasteful period in modern history and say yes to the most resourceful period in history. ✠

An 80-pound Copi caught from the Red River-Louisiana. Imagine a giant fish of that size flying through the air and landing in your boat! Out of this monster fish, you can easily make fish tacos to feed twenty people!

WHY EAT INVASIVE CARP?
ROY BRABHAM, M.D.

TACKLING INVASIVE AND NUISANCE SPECIES

"I consider [invasive] carp to be an excellent food source for a number of reasons. Like all fish, it delivers a lot of protein and healthy fats. Unlike ocean fish, sustainability is not an issue with [invasive] carp. It is overrunning the central American waterways, making it a nuisance and crowding out [native] species. It feeds on plankton, which is at the bottom of the food chain. This means that progressive food chain concentration of harmful chemicals, such as dioxin and PCBs, and heavy metals such as mercury, does not occur in [invasive] carp like it does in carnivorous/omnivorous fish. Some would argue that farm-raised fish, like catfish and Tilapia, avoid the food chain accumulation of toxic substances. But this is not necessarily the case, as such farmed fish are typically fed fish-meal derived from fish that are subject to these kinds of contamination.

Many farmed fish are also given grain-based feeds. This reduces the levels of omega-3 fats and increases the amounts of omega-6 fats in their flesh. Since a proper balance of omega-3's to omega-6's is required for proper regulation of inflammation processes and thus good health, the imbalances in grain-fed farmed fish are counterproductive, particularly since most people already have too little omega-3 and too much omega-6 intake.

Another problem with farmed fish lies in the fact that large numbers of these fish are crammed into ponds or pens. This is similar to the concentrated animal-feeding operations such as those used for chickens. These conditions promote growth of pathogens like bacteria, yeasts, and parasites as well as significant amounts of antibiotics. In addition, significant amounts of antibiotics and pesticides are needed to avoid infection issues. This can result in issues such as emergence of antibiotic-resistant organisms and disruption of normal bacterial balance in the digestive tracts of consumers. The crowded conditions can also create problems with accumulation of excrement and even dead fish material. This is reduced by filtering and recirculating the water (assuming these are done), but some contamination from these sources will remain." ✠

Chef Philippe says, "My close friend and commercial fisherman Clint Carter (pictured left) nets **Copi***, aka invasive carp, in the upper Mississippi River. These invaders plague the Wildlife and Fisheries policymakers across the entire Mississippi Basin."*

MONTEREY BAY AQUARIUM
Seafood WATCH®

Invasive Carp was Added to the Monterey Bay Aquarium Seafood Watch List In September 2019 as a SUSTAINABLE FOOD SOURCE

Tackling Invasive and Nuisance Species

THE MISSISSIPPI RIVER BASIN: 1.5 MILLION MILES OF RIVER

Photo: A more accurate Map of the Mississippi River Basin Made by Shannon1 using USGS data. Reprinted under the GNU Free Documentation License Version 1.2 or later found at https://en.wikipedia.org/wiki/en:GNU_Free_Documentation_License.

    This map shows only the major tributaries of the Mississippi River. The Mississippi River Basin covers over two-thirds of the United States with a whopping approximately 1.5 million river miles. It is home to most invasive species, including the destructive, Invasive Carp. These carp colonized every inch of those river miles, and in some cases, they are up to 90% of the biomass, which leaves room for very few native fish species. They harm the entire Mississippi River Basin ecosystem, including water quality, recreational and commercial fishing, waterfowl, hunting, and water sports activities.

"WELL CHEF, THEY SURE JUMPED IN THE WRONG BOAT"

TACKLING INVASIVE AND NUISANCE SPECIES

My dear friend, famed outdoorsman Don Dubuc (l) of the radio and television show Bayou Wild, and his co-host, Martha Spencer (r), held an alligator gar that made great fish gar balls a Louisiana delicacy.

When on Don Dubuc's radio show discussing my first encounter with invasive Carp, he went on saying, "Well, Chef, they sure jumped in the wrong boat!" I've known Don for years, and we cooked and served a variety of invasive species in many charity events supporting education to preserve wildlife habitats.

I have cooked in several shows on his television network, Bayou Wild, promoting the edibility of diverse invasive species. There is no better voice supporting wildlife habitat preservation. I am fortunate and proud to be his friend.

Don Dubuc is not the only one. There are sports and outdoors personalities and advocates all over the United States who actively support preservation of natural habitats and in many different ways. Explore local resources such as your state Wildlife and Fisheries agency or similar organizations to find out what invasive species are in your area and what rules regulations might be in place regarding them. You are sure to find one or more species that are edible and you, like me, can practice the **Can't Beat 'Em, Eat 'Em** philosophy. ✠

Tackling Invasive and Nuisance Species

INVASIVE CARP AKA *COPI* RECIPE PLACES 3RD IN NOLA NAVY COOK-OFF

In April of 2022, New Orleans, Louisiana was host to NOLA Navy Week and its favored Louisiana Seafood Cook-Off. During this iconic event, Naval culinary specialists, who spend most of their time at sea, from the United States and France are paired with local land-based chefs for a Louisiana seafood competition like no other. Once the incredible U.S. and French Navy ships dock in the Crescent City, the chefs pair off for the event on the Riverwalk at the Spanish Plaza.

The event is not only a fun culinary showdown but also serves to raise awareness about Louisiana's incredible salt and fresh water seafood as well as bring attention to the successes and needs of Louisiana's huge commercial seafood industry and the problems it faces with natural disasters and invasive species. Chef Philippe Parola participates in this event as often as he can.

At the 2022 competition, Chef Philippe was paired with Seaman Commissary Man Striker Lemuel Corpuz of the USS Lassen, a U.S. Navy guided missile destroyer. These two chefs chose to use INVASIVE CARP and delicious Louisiana crawfish (which is also an invasive species in some U.S. states). ! The recipe (shown right) WON THIRD PLACE in the competition against prime seafood such as grouper, tuna, and blue crab. It was the first time an invasive species has placed in the top three in a cook-off!

Above: On my left, Navy Chef Lemuel Corpuz, from the USS Lassen, a Naval destroyer, was my partner chef in the U. S. Navy Cook-Off. The COPI (invasive carp) recipe we cooked won third place.

Below: Chef Philippe having the time of his life with an enthusiastic crowd of fans in New Orleans at the U. S. Navy Seafood Cook-Off event. Invasive carp aka COPI placed third in the competition. It was the first time an invasive species won in a cook-off.

Chef Philippe's Invasive Carp aka COPI Navy Cook-Off Recipe

TACKLING INVASIVE AND NUISANCE SPECIES

Ingredients

3 oz	Silver Carp aka COPI Filet (9 Servings)
1 lb	Louisiana Crawfish Tails and 9 Boiled Crawfish For Garnish
12 oz	Fresh Spinach
4 oz	Olive Oil
1 oz	Chopped Garlic
3 oz	Homemade Cajun Seasoning
4 oz	Granulated Louisiana Sugar Cane
4 oz	White Wine
2 oz	Fresh Squeezed Lemon Juice
8 oz	Sour Cream
1 tsp	Louisiana Hot Sauce

Cooking Instructions

1. Heat up 3 oz olive oil in a skillet to smoking point then saute seasoned silver carp filets with Cajun seasoning over medium high heat until light golden color.

2. Sprinkle granulated sugar cane over golden silver carp filets; continue to pan saute over medium heat until fully cooked.

3. Remove filets and deglaze with white wine and fresh squeezed lemon juice then saute crawfish tails for 2 minutes and remove tails to a bowl.

4. Add sour cream. Mix and reduce until sauce has smooth consistency then correct seasoning to taste if needed.

5. In a separate skillet, saute spinach with 1 oz olive oil and garlic until fully cooked.

6. Display a bed of sautéed spinach in serving plate, then fish filets topped with crawfish tails and sauce. Garnish with boiled crawfish.

The top-three winning dish featuring invasive carp and red crawfish which is also invasive in some U.S. states.

Chef Philippe with United States and French Navy seamen at the NOLA Navy Week Louisiana Seafood Cook-Off holding a 45 pound invasive carp.

Tackling Invasive and Nuisance Species

A CRAWFISH TALE: FROM MUD BUGS TO MULTI-MILLIONS

Let's start with a fish story—a crawfish tale, not to be mistaken for the edible, delicious crawfish tail. In Louisiana, red crawfish, aka swamp crawfish (bugs), are indigenous to our area.

But, in November 2022, the Department of Natural Resources in Wisconsin announced its first criminal conviction under the state's invasive species law. A Louisiana company was found guilty and paid significant fines for exporting red crawfish to their state.

Simultaneously, Michigan and Minnesota are actively seeking to prevent an invasion of the swamp crawfish.

Remember, as the saying goes, at your next crawfish boil, "one man's trash is another man's treasure."

In Wisconsin, it is not about the appealing taste or spices. It's about the prevention of an invasive species wreaking havoc on the ecosystem of those areas in which Louisiana crawfish threaten the ecosystem in the upper Midwest.

By contrast to the upper Midwest states, Louisiana fishermen have been harvesting indigenous crawfish for over a century. After World War II, rice farmers saw a great opportunity and started farming crawfish.

Farm-raised and wild-caught crawfish now make the Cajun- delicacy a year-round proposition. According to the Louisiana Department of Wildlife and Fisheries, there are more than 1,000 crawfish fishermen and more than 1,300 crawfish farmers.

Louisiana produces over 120 million pounds of crawfish annually. Louisiana's crawfish industry contributes more than $400 million annually to the state's economy. That's a lot of treasure coming from someone else's trash.

This should serve as just one example of how an invasive or nuisance species can be turned into a thriving, profitable commercial industry when approached with the right kind of mindset and appropriate motivation.

The various species of invasive carp cause significant problems across the Mississippi River Basin. It is getting worse.

Imagine, however, that by harvesting invasive carp and turning it into a wonderful protein source, it too might become a multi-million dollar industry, creating jobs and expanding the economies of various states.

As important as that could be for the economy, the possibility of feeding malnourished children or hungry elderly worldwide is even more exciting.

Famous Louisiana Boiled Crawfish

Tackling Invasive and Nuisance Species

Dr. Dawn Aubrey (left) and Chef Philippe Parola (right) attending the NACUFS* Annual Convention in Rhode Island. Dr. Dawn Aubrey has been a huge supporter and promoter of the Can't Beat 'Em, Eat 'Em campaign. She was instrumental in placing the first ever invasive species, Copi (aka invasive carp), on the menu in university dining halls.

* National Association of College and University Food Services

Kit Smith, Director of Residential Dining at Rensselaer Polytechnic Institute. Kit is a continuing supporter of Can't Beat 'Em, Eat 'Em. His efforts and support are hugely appreciated by all who are concerned with the threat of invasive carp.

Kevin Irons, Aquatic Nuisance Species Program Manager, Illinois Department of Natural Resources. Chef Philippe has worked with Kevin for nearly 10 years promoting the edibility of invasive carp. He is also the force behind the new name "COPI".

TACKLING INVASIVE AND NUISANCE SPECIES

Louisiana and Illinois Find [Invasive] Carp Solution with "Can't Beat 'Em, Eat 'Em" Campaign

by Ewell Smith, Gulf Seafood Foundation Board Member

Invasive Carp, rebranded as Silverfin, is a fish everyone can learn to love including Illinois Lt. Gov. Evelyn Sanguinetti. She joined Louisiana Chef Philippe Parola and other partners from Illinois and Louisiana at a January luncheon in Champaign to showcase and encourage the human consumption of invasive carp as a healthy food source in America. Photo: Ewell Smith/Gulf Seafood Foundation

From the Gulf to the Great Lakes, from Denver to Knoxville, Bighead and Silver carp have overtaken manmade lakes and large sections of rivers threatening the ecosystem and the multi-million dollar recreational and commercial fishing industry.

These two carps are invasive species introduced into fish farm ponds in the central Midwest in the 1970's to clean murky pond water. Flooding along the Missouri and Mississippi Rivers caused ponds to overflow, allowing the carp to escape into rivers and reproduce in the wild.

Eight years ago, Louisiana Chef Philippe Parola approached the Louisiana Seafood Promotion and Marketing Board expressing his concern for native species of fish in Louisiana and the Gulf threatened by the rapidly growing numbers of invasive carp, a fish with few predators to population growth. A single female can produce up to one million eggs per year. If left unchecked the impact could severely damage recreational fishing, tourism, and the watersports industry up and down the Mississippi.

The threat of the possibility of the invasive carp's ability to thrive in the brackish estuaries forming Louisiana's coastline raised the fear the fish could decimate the state's coastal fishing industry. Shrimp, oyster, blue crab and other finfish all rely on those plankton-rich waters during some point in their life cycle, but if invasive carp establish a population, they could damage the already fragile ecosystem.

Chef Parola serves a Silverfin dish to a Tulane University student. The school is working the with the two-state partnership to regularly serve the fish to students. The Louisiana Seafood exchange is the first distributor of the fish in Louisiana. Photo: Ewell Smith/Gulf Seafood Foundation

"In our state, these fish grow 30 to 50 pounds on average," said the Chef. "They can eat their weight in plankton in a day. After invading an area they annihilate the vital plant food local indigenous seafood relies upon."

To date the federal government has spent hundreds of millions of dollars building electrical fence and has tried to poison the fish in an attempt to keep the fish out of the Great Lakes and rivers.

To ensure the survival of native species, Chef Parola decide to find a solution for the rapidly growing problem. If you can't beat them, eat them.

The flesh of invasive carp is light, mild and flaky, akin to delicate crabmeat. The problem is the fish suffers from a serious image problem: people confuse invasive carp with the common bottom-feeding carp that has a stronger, fishier flavor.

Illinois River: Invasive Silver carp jump out of the water after being disturbed by sounds of watercraft. The invasive species, which can reach four-feet in length and weigh up to 100 pounds, wreak havoc on native fish by gobbling up plankton. Photo: Illinois River Biological Station/ Nerissa Michaels

This is a reprinted article from the Gulf Seafood Foundation's "The Voice of the Gulf" Newsroom website and is Copyright © 2022 Gulf Seafood News with All Rights Reserved in accordance with International Copyright Law. This article has been reprinted with full permissions from the copyright owner.

Tackling Invasive and Nuisance Species

Chef Parola explains the importance of Silverfin to Eric Bucker (middle) Sysco's Senior Director of Seafood and Kevin Easter, Seafood Product Manager, at the company's headquarters in Houston. Photo: Ewell Smith/Gulf Seafood Foundation

As Chef Paul Prudhomme did in the 1980's with the then unwanted Red fish by serving it blackened, to overcome the negative associations Chef Parola is marketing invasive carp for consumption as Silverfin.

"[Invasive] carp has incredibly complex bone structure, which makes it very difficult to clean. People mistakenly think it is a 'trash fish', but it is not," said the Chef. "One thing we know how to do in Louisiana, and do extremely well, is cook."

Parola's mission is not only to preach the delicious virtues of Silverfin, but also to pave the way for creating a sustainable fish and food processing plant that can support a commercial invasive carp fishing industry. To complete the Chef's vision, a change in fishery regulations to remove catch limits is needed.

The Chef has traveled the Mississippi River, from Louisiana to Illinois, the past 8 years meeting with environmentalist, government officials, fishermen, media and investors. "By bringing Silverfin to market we can help balance the consumption of plankton by the fish making it possible for our native species to co-exist," he explained.

Failing to have the current capacity to process the fish in the U.S., the bone-riddled fish is currently being sent to Vietnam to have bones removed by hand. The cleaned fish is then returned to the U.S. to be sold to restaurants, educational institutions and grocery outlets.

"[Invasive] carp will be a very profitable for the commercial fishermen at current prices," said Louisiana fisherman Richard Durrett who has been working closely with the Chef in bringing the fish to market. "The Atchafalaya and Mississippi River is overflowing with the fish. In four hours I can easily catch more than 47,000 lbs."

Chef Parola's untiring efforts are starting to bear fruit. In Illinois, The Department of Commerce and Economic Opportunity is set to review details for two possible sites for Silverfin processing plants that would process 50,000 to 100,000 pounds of fish per day.

In the Bayou State, both Governor John Bell Edwards and Lieutenant Governor Billy Nungesser, along with the Secretary of Wildlife and Fisheries, Jack Montoucet, recognize the threat of the invasive fish and support Parola's efforts. In addition, Sodexo, a company providing catering and facilities management to 100 million consumers daily in 56 countries, has expressed interest in distributing the fish nationwide.

Representatives from Illinois, ground zero for this issue with more than 15,500 Silverfin per river mile, and Louisiana met at a January luncheon in Champaign, IL to kick off the "Cant Beat Em' Eat Em" campaign, which showcased the fish and encouraged its consumption as a healthy food source. This first-of-its-kind project is an

"Invasive carp will be a very profitable for the commercial fishermen at current prices," said Louisiana fisherman Richard Durrett while fishing on the Atchafalaya River's control structures where water is diverted from the Mississippi River. Photo: Richard Durrett

This is a reprinted article from the Gulf Seafood Foundation's "The Voice of the Gulf" Newsroom website and is Copyright © 2022 Gulf Seafood News with All Rights Reserved in accordance with International Copyright Law. This article has been reprinted with full permissions from the copyright owner.

Tackling Invasive and Nuisance Species

Representatives from Illinois and Louisiana met at a January luncheon in Champaign to kick off the "Cant Beat Em' Eat Em" campaign, which showcased the fish and encouraged its consumption as a healthy food source. Photo: University of Illinois

alliance of two States, as well as the University of Illinois, which serves as a liaison.

According to the Chef the "Cant Beat Em' Eat Em" campaign can have a positive ecological and economic impact for both states.

"We are very proud of the hard work our partners have done to educate the public about the delicious and healthy consumption of invasive Carp and to help fishermen to sell it, become financially viable and increase its demand," said Illinois Lt. Governor Sanguinetti. "This effort will potentially help grow our fishery industry and create jobs while at the same time reduce the population of invasive invasive Carp and help prevent further spread."

In a statement Louisiana Lt. Governor Billy Nungesser, whose office oversees the Louisiana Seafood Board, said, "We are excited to partner with the University of Illinois, the Illinois Department of Natural Resources and Chef Philippe Parola in finding a workable and sustainable solution to the growing threat of the invasive carp. This is a coordinated effort to create a whole new fishing industry to reduce the threat invasive carp poses to our own vital fishing industry and ecosystem."

Invasive carp can be a great source of food because it is low in sodium as well as a good source of vitamin B12, selenium, protein, phosphorous and Omega-3 and Omega-6 fatty acids.

"It is wild caught, sustainable, and a natural protein. This is the beginning of the end regarding the threat this fish presents to the Mississippi River Ecosystem from Illinois to Louisiana," said Chef Parola at the event.

Chef Phillippe Parola educates Lieutenant Governor Billy Nungesser on the difficulties of de-boning the invasive carp. Bringing the great tasting fish to market as Silverfin can be a win-win for everyone. Photo: Ewell Smith/Gulf Seafood Foundation

"The solution to the millions of invasive carp may rest not in government engineering projects alone, but in private enterprise and old-fashioned marketing," according to the Louisiana Lt. Governor. "By addressing the invasive carp issue we are helping to protect our native species, while creating jobs for our fishermen by bringing this fish to market. Why eat imported catfish from Vietnam when our restaurants can offer delicious Silverfin dishes?"

This is a reprinted article from the Gulf Seafood Foundation's "The Voice of the Gulf" Newsroom website and is Copyright © 2022 Gulf Seafood News with All Rights Reserved in accordance with International Copyright Law. This article has been reprinted with full permissions from the copyright owner.

Tackling Invasive and Nuisance Species

AS CHEF PHILIPPE ALWAYS SAYS: CAN'T BEAT 'EM, EAT 'EM!

As you read about the invaders, think about their impact on ecosystems and consider the opportunities we have to protect our environment by minimizing damages caused by these species. Then rethink wasting millions of pounds of perfectly edible proteins while at the same time humanely controlling populations of species and saving those upon which the invaders prey. Contemplate the benefits of not broadcasting pesticides to control edible, flavorsome plant species. Since invasive species are highly prolific reproducers, they are a sustainable food source that can persist for many future generations..

Hopefully, this will lead you to the conclusion that I long ago reached, allowing you to shift your paradigm about nature's gifts. ✠

Invasive carp was originally processed as a delicious Fish Cake

Eradication for many invasive species is impossible but i am certain that the best way to control the problem is living by my motto...

IF YOU CAN'T BEAT 'EM... EAT 'EM!!

What a fantastic day! The Seattle Seahawks hosted us. Outside the stadium with the entire kitchen staff, I am promoting the first Invasive Carp served in a sports arena concession. To my immediate left, above the lady holding the box of Silverfin Fish Cakes, is Mike Johnson—my former chef apprentice, now the executive chef of the LSU Athletics Department.

Tackling Invasive and Nuisance Species

My young friend, Hugo Sdralek, was a French tourist in Louisiana, visiting from the town of Ebreuil near where I grew up. He was so excited to land a whopper of a black drum in brackish waters of coastal Louisiana that he lit up a cigar! The invasive carp are now adapting to brackish waters and thus threaten recreational fishing in gulf states.

Chef Philippe says: "I encountered the first invasive carp fishing for this Alligator Gar Fish for Jeff Corwin's Extreme Cuisine episode on Food Network. I enjoyed working with the charismatic Jeff Corwin."

Chef Philippe purchasing invasive carp direct from Rusty Kimball and another commercial fishermen in Louisiana

Hungry people lined up and eager to get a taste of invasive carp prepared by Chef Philippe at the New Orleans "Beast Feast" festival in the Spring of 2018.

Tackling Invasive and Nuisance Species

Louisiana Governor John Bel Edwards, third left, accepts my gift of a "Can't Beat 'Em, Eat 'Em" T-shirt. We were joined by Wildlife & Fisheries Secretary Jack Montoucet, second left, and Ewell Smith, left, formerly the Executive Director of the Louisiana Seafood Promotion Board.

Chef Philippe with Louisiana's promoter general, Lt. Governor Billy Nungesser (c), and his wife Cher (l). Lt. Governor Nungesser is the force behind promoting our Louisiana seafood products and bringing tourists to our state. Lt. Governor Nungesser has also been an avid supporter of our Can't Beat 'Em, Eat 'Em campaign.

Chef Philippe has visited numerous colleges and universities to talk about invasive carp and other invasive species. These visits, as often as possible, include serving an invasive carp food dish in one of the school's cafeterias. These servings are always a huge success and usually result in students coming back for seconds or even thirds (especially the athletes!). In the above photo, Chef Philippe is serving Copi (invasive carp) fish cakes to students at Tulane University in New Orleans, Louisiana.

Chef Philippe in Pierre Part, Louisiana, getting to spend time with the legendary alligator hunter Troy Landry of Swamp People television fame.

Chef Philippe, with renowned television series host Jeremy Wade of River Monsters, is on break from location filming the documentary 'Mighty Mississippi.'

RECIPES FOR INVASIVE FISH SPECIES
FRESH WATER FISH ⚓ SALT WATER FISH

SILVER CARP AKA COPI

INVASIVE SPECIES PROFILE

Geography. The silver carp is native to major Pacific waters in eastern Asia — from the Amur River of far east Russia, South through most of China to the Pearl River and northern Vietnam.

Description. Silver carp are deep-bodied, laterally compressed fish that are silver in color when young and turn a shade of green on the back to silver on the belly when mature. Silver carp have tiny scales on the body but no scales on their head or gills. They have a large mouth with no teeth in the jaw but, instead, have teeth back in the throat. Their eyes are very close to the front of the body's mid-line and are slightly turned downward.

Jumping Carp. Silver carp are easily disturbed and jump up to 10 feet into the air in response to almost any noise, like rocks thrown in the water, geese taking off from the water, or outboard motors. Sometimes they land in boats and strike passengers.

Threat. When a boat goes more than 20 mph, a fish weighing over 20 pounds can damage the boat or, worse, cause serious injury to passengers. Water skiing and other recreational water sports have become dangerous in areas where silver carp are found.

In addition to the threat to boaters and water sports enthusiasts, silver carp push out native species by taking their space and eating their food thereby disrupting entire aquatic ecosystems.

COPI (SILVER CARP) FISH CAKES
SERVES 4

INGREDIENTS

3 lbs.	Silver carp fillet
½ cup	Water
1 ea.	1 egg, beaten
½ cup	Mayonnaise
¼ cup	Sour cream
¼ cup	Onion, raw, diced
¼ cup	Celery, diced
4 oz.	Butter, unsalted
1 cup	Breadcrumbs
4 oz.	Breadcrumbs
To Taste	Hot & spicy mayonnaise or dipping sauce
To Taste	Seasoning to taste

COOKING INSTRUCTIONS

» Preheat oven to 325° F

» Place ½ cup water in the baking pan

» Place silver carp fillets in the pan with the water

» Bake at 325° F for 15 minutes or until fully cooked

» Remove from oven when fully cooked. Remove bones

» Add cooked fish to a bowl with egg, regular mayonnaise, sour cream, onion, celery, butter, breadcrumbs, and seasoning to taste.

» Mix well

» Place the mixture in the refrigerator, covered overnight

» Preheat oven to 350° F

» Form mixture into patties 3-4 inches wide, ½ inch thick

» Bake patties at 350° F until fully cooked to a golden brown

» Serve with hot & spicy mayonnaise or other dipping sauce

THIS RECIPE CAN BE USED WITH ANY TYPE OF INVASIVE CARP!

BROWN TROUT

INVASIVE SPECIES PROFILE

Geography. The brown trout are native to Iceland, Europe, Western Asia, and Northwestern Africa. They are very adaptable and now occur on every major continent except Antarctica. Brown trout are primarily a fresh water fish but easily adapt to brackish and salt waters.

Description. This freshwater fish is usually brown, brownish-yellow, or olive in color. They typically have darker spots along their flanks. Their caudal fin is somewhat square-shaped and does not have spots. They can grow to a little over two feet long and weigh up to 10 pounds.

Threat. Brown trout are large fish that are highly predatory. They grow larger and faster than most native fish species, especially other types of trout. They are a huge threat to native fish species, especially when they are invasive in small fresh water streams. They will eat nearly any living creature in the waters they inhabit. Therefore, they not only eat native fish but also eat other fish that are the usual food source for native fish.

Brown trout are also prolific breeders. Their sheer numbers can push out native species.

The brown trout has been nominated by more than one global organization as one of the "100 of the World's Worst Invasive Species".

Photo: Helge Busch-Paulick (Grand-Duc @ Wikipedia) under the GNU Free Documentation License found at https://en.wikipedia.org/wiki/en:GNU_Free_Documentation_License

BROWN TROUT PECAN
SERVES 4

INGREDIENTS

4 ea	Brown trout fillets
4 oz	Butter, unsalted
½ cup	Pecan halves
¼ cup	White wine
2 oz	Lemon juice
2 tbsp	Cilantro, chopped
Per Taste	Seasoning to taste

COOKING INSTRUCTIONS

» Season trout fillets to taste

» In a sauté skillet, heat butter till light golden brown

» Sauté trout for 3 minutes on each side on medium heat or until fully cooked

» Remove the fish and place it on a platter

» Sauté pecans until crisp (do not burn) in remaining butter

» Add cilantro continue to sauté for 1 minute

» Add lemon juice and stir well

» Top trout with pecans, lemon cilantro lemon butter sauce from the pan

» Serve hot with side dishes

BLACK CARP AKA COPI

INVASIVE SPECIES PROFILE

Geography. The black carp is native to major Pacific waters in eastern Asia—from the Amur River of far East Russia, South through most of China to the Pearl River and Northern Vietnam.

Description. The black carp looks a lot like grass carp with similar body shape, size, and placement of fins. They both have large scales, but the black carp scales are darker (not black), and their pharyngeal teeth are large and look similar to human molars. Black carp also have a longer snout than grass carp.

Black carp can also grow substantially more significantly larger than other species of invasive carp — known to grow up to five feet long and as much as 150 pounds.

Threat. Unlike the grass carp, the Black carp has not been detected in the Great Lakes even though they have been identified in the state of Illinois,. There is fear among experts it could be introduced from there. This is disconcerting because of the carp's reproduction rates, potentially leading to a large population in a very short period of time.

Black carp have also been reported in Arkansas, Louisiana, Kentucky, Mississippi, and other southern and eastern states..

These carp require large rivers to reproduce. They eat mussels and snails, freshwater shrimp, crayfish, and insects.

CAJUN STYLE BLACK CARP
SERVES 8

INGREDIENTS

4 lbs	Black carp fillets
4 ea	Tomatoes, sliced
2 ea	Onions, sliced
4 ea	Garlic, chopped
½ cup	White wine
2 oz	Lemon juice
4 oz	Unsalted butter
¼ cup	Parmesan cheese, grated
Per Serving	Steamed Rice
Per Taste	Cajun seasoning to taste

COOKING INSTRUCTIONS

- » Preheat oven to 325° F.
- » Season black carp fillets to taste and place filets in a baking pan with butter
- » Bake for 5 minutes
- » Remove pan; add white wine and lemon juice over fillets
- » Evenly place onion, garlic, sliced tomatoes, and Parmesan cheese on top of the fillets
- » Bake for 10 minutes
- » Serve over steam rice.

THIS RECIPE CAN BE USED WITH ANY TYPE OF INVASIVE CARP!

LIONFISH

INVASIVE SPECIES PROFILE

Geography. The lionfish is native throughout the South Pacific and Indian Oceans, ranging from Australia to French Polynesia to Southern Asia. They are primarily invasive along the Southern coast of the United States along the Gulf of Mexico. Invasive lionfish were introduced into U.S., coastal waters due to releases into the wild by pet owners.

Description. They are white or cream colored and have alternating thick and thin, red or brown, vertical stripes along the body and the head. Sometimes, their vertical lines merge along the fish's flank to form a "V" shape. They have fan-like pectoral fins and long separated dorsal spines.

Threat. Lionfish are primarily fish-eaters with few predators outside of their natural habitat. Their presence can hurt commercial and recreational fishing.

Increases in the population of invasive lionfish cause great amounts of additional stress on coral reefs and other marine ecosystems because Lionfish eat herbivores that eat algae from the reefs. That means the coral reef is susceptible to harmful algae growth which creates an imbalance in the ecosystem.

These very fragile aquatic ecosystems are already under great stress due to climate change, pollution, and other environmental stresses. The last thing these ecosystems need is a threat as huge as that posed by invasive lionfish.

LIONFISH MEUNIÈRE
SERVES 2

INGREDIENTS

2 ea.	Lionfish fillets
2 tbsp	Olive oil
2 oz	Butter, unsalted, melted
1 tbsp	Garlic, minced
2 tbsp	Cilantro, chopped
1 tbsp	Lemon juice
2 tbsp	White wine
Per Taste	Seasoning to taste

COOKING INSTRUCTIONS

» Preheat oven to 350° F
» Season Lionfish fillets to taste and place into baking pan
» Evenly coat with olive oil and melted butter
» Bake Lionfish fillets for 5 minutes at 350° F
» Remove from oven and pour white wine and lemon juice over fillets
» Evenly top garlic and cilantro over fillets
» Return to oven and bake 350° F for 5 minutes or until fully cooked
» Serve hot with sauce from the pan drizzled over the fillets and your favorite side dishes

INVASIVE SPECIES RECIPE

ARMORED SAILFIN CATFISH

INVASIVE SPECIES PROFILE

Geography. The armored sailfin catfish, commonly known as plecos, is native to central and south America, especially in the Amazon River Basin. They have become invasive primarily due to aquarium dumping through the pet trade industry.

Description. The armored catfish have a sucker on the underside of its head that is used to attach itself to many surfaces. Their adipose fin has a spine that supports it upward, and their pectoral fins have thick, smaller, toothed spines. They have rows of bony plates covering all of their body except the belly, and they have a dark "spotted" or "worm-like" pattern that marks their dark golden bodies.

Threat. The armored sailfin catfish is especially problematic in Florida and Texas. When released into the wild, this fish can grow up to three feet long.

Its destructive behavior contributes to the erosion of stream banks because these fish are cavity nesters that dig deep burrows, which can cause banks to collapse. These weakened banks and levees are also a hazard to fishermen and other outdoorsmen.

The overabundance of armored sailfin catfish in invaded freshwater ecosystems causes a reduction in native fish species because the armored catfish out-competes them for food and space.

ARMORED CATFISH IN WINE AND CAPERS
SERVES 2

INGREDIENTS

2 ea	Armored catfish fillet
½ cup	Flour
2 tbsp	Olive oil
2 tbsp	Capers
4 tbsp	White wine
1 tbsp	Lemon juice
Per Taste	Seasoning to taste

COOKING INSTRUCTIONS

- Season fillets to taste
- Coat the fillet evenly with flour
- Put olive oil in a sauté pan and heat on medium-high heat
- Sauté fillets until golden brown for 3 minutes on each side or until fully cooked
- Remove fish fillets
- Add capers into remaining olive oil, sauté capers for 30 seconds
- Add white wine and lemon juice to the pan with capers
- Reduce the sauce on medium-high heat for 1 minute
- Top-cooked fish fillet with white wine caper sauce
- Serve hot

THIS RECIPE CAN BE USED WITH ANY TYPE OF INVASIVE CARP!

INVASIVE SPECIES RECIPE

TILAPIA

INVASIVE SPECIES PROFILE

Geography. Multiple species of Tilapia fish are invasive, including the Nile and Blue Tilapia. Tilapia are native to Africa, where they are farmed for food. They are also farmed in Asia.

Description. Nile Tilapia are brown or gray with soft banding on their body. Their tail is vertically striped. The blue Tilapia is bluer or blue-gray in color and is similarly striped but has a red edge to its dorsal fin. Both species have spiny top fins. Females who are breeding have orange edges on their dorsal and caudal fins.

Adult Tilapia are usually 5 - 8 inches in length and weigh 5 - 8 pounds. The largest specimen found in the wild was right at 21 inches and weighed in at over 10 pounds.

Threat. In fresh water ecosystems where invasive Tilapia are present, a significant diminishing of plant, fish and shrimp species has been recorded. Experts also believe that Blue Tilapia is also responsible for unionid mussel declines in the state of Texas.

The adaptability of the Tilapia, especially with its wide range of temperature toleration, allow it to firmly establish itself in waters throughout the southern states along the Gulf of Mexico.

The Tilapia is considered a significant threat to the spawning areas, food, and habitat space of native species.

SOUTHERN BAKED TILAPIA
SERVES 2

INGREDIENTS

4 ea.	Invasive Tilapia fillet
1 cup	Marinara tomato sauce
4 tbsp	Olive oil
¼ cup	Fresh basil, chopped
¼ cup	Red onion, finely chopped
For 4	Cooked pasta of choice
Per Taste	Season to taste

INVASIVE SPECIES RECIPE

COOKING INSTRUCTIONS

» Preheat oven to 350° F
» Season Tilapia fillets to taste
» Coat the baking pan with olive oil
» Place seasoned Tilapia fillets in the baking pan with olive oil
» Coat fillets evenly with onion and basil
» Pour marinara sauce over the fillets
» Bake at 350° F for 15 minutes or until fully cooked
» Serve over cooked pasta

NORTHERN SNAKEHEAD FISH

INVASIVE SPECIES PROFILE

Geography. The Northern Snakehead fish is native to China, Korea, and Russia. The first snakeheads were found in the United States in Maryland in 2002, where a local family released them as a symbolic gesture of thanks for a family member being healed of a severe illness.

Description. Northern snakehead fish live in fresh water ponds, lakes, streams, rivers, wetlands, and ponds. They have an elongated body that can grow to nearly 4 feet in length. They are usually tan, dark brown, or black in color and have a mottled, snake-like pattern all over their bodies. They also have a long dorsal fin along most of their bodies on their backs. They have a large mouth, a protruding lower jaw, and many teeth..

Threat. Northern snakehead fish are strong predators who prey on small fish and crustaceans, small amphibians, reptiles, and even some birds and mammals. They become aggressive feeders during the juvenile stage and continue to be aggressive through adulthood. During spawning season, they become even more aggressive than usual and are detrimental to the balance of the ecosystems in which they are invasive.

It is estimated that if the Northern Snakehead fish becomes fully established in United States waters, it could cost millions of dollars in management, plus ecological and recreational damage.

SNAKEHEAD FISH ALMONDINE
SERVES 4

INGREDIENTS

4 ea	Northern snakehead fish fillets
2 oz	Butter, unsalted, melted
2 oz	Lemon juice
1 oz	Garlic, chopped
1 oz	Cilantro, chopped
½ cup	Almonds toasted
Per Taste	Seasoning to taste

COOKING INSTRUCTIONS

» Season fish fillet to taste
» In a sauté pan, heat butter on medium-high heat until light brown
» Sauté fish, frequently turning until fully cooked
» Remove cooked fish from the pan
» Add garlic and cilantro into hot butter in the pan
» Sauté for 30 seconds
» Add lemon juice into the butter sauce
» Plate hot fish fillets
» Pour evenly garlic-lemon butter sauce over cooked fillets
» Top with toasted almonds

INVASIVE SPECIES RECIPE

GRASS CARP AKA COPI

INVASIVE SPECIES PROFILE

Geography. The grass carp is native to major Pacific waters in eastern Asia from the Amur River of far eastern Russian south through most of China to the Pearl River and northern Vietnam. Soon after their arrival in the United States, several grass carp escaped into the Mississippi River basin during flooding. They have since spread throughout the entire Mississippi River valley through tributaries and estuaries.

Description. It is a large member of the minnow family and has a slightly laterally compressed body with its mouth at the bottom end of a wide head and small eyes that are low on the head. It is olive-brown on the dorsal side with a white belly and sides with dark-edged, silver scales. Its dorsal fin is toward the back of the body. It can reach lengths of more than five feet and weigh more than 80 lbs. It is the grass carp that creates major issues in the Great Lakes States. It thrives in quiet, shallow waters.

Threat. The size of grass carp allows each of them to consume between 20% and 100% of their body weight per day. So, grass carp consume massive amounts of aquatic vegetation, in direct competition with native fish, waterfowl, and invertebrate species in the areas where grass carp are invasive. This creates a massive disruption to the ecosystem which results in a great loss of habitat for native aquatic and semi-aquatic wildlife.

GRASS CARP AU GRATIN
SERVES 6 - 8

INGREDIENTS

10-12 lbs	Grass carp, whole, gutted, beheaded, butterflied
2 cups	Heavy cream
1 cup	Parmesan cheese, grated
2 cups	Cheddar cheese, shredded
To Taste	Seasoning to taste

COOKING INSTRUCTIONS

» Season butterfly grass carp and place skin down on the BBQ pit
» Cook on medium-high heat for 35 minutes or until fully cooked
» Remove from the cooking surface
» Remove bones by hand and place cooked meat in a baking pan
» Preheat oven to 350° F
» In a separate bowl, mix Parmesan cheese with heavy cream and season to taste
» Pour cream and cheese mixture over fish meat
» Top with shredded cheddar cheese
» Bake for 10 minutes or until cheese is melted
» Serve hot

INVASIVE SPECIES RECIPE

THIS RECIPE CAN BE USED WITH COMMON CARP!

SWAMP EEL

INVASIVE SPECIES PROFILE

Geography. The swamp eel is native to India, Myanmar, China, Thailand, Cambodia, Laos, Vietnam, Hong Kong, Japan, Taiwan, Malaysia, Indonesia, the Philippines, and Australia. They are currently present in several U.S. states including Florida, Georgia, Hawaii, New Jersey and others. These invasive eels are believed to have been introduced into the wild through aquarium dumping and fish market release.

Description. They are usually dark brown or green in color and look similar to the American Eels, lampreys, and salamanders (without the legs). The swamp eel differs from other eels because they do not have pectoral fins. They differ from lampreys in that the swamp eel gills are a single V-shaped opening, while lampreys have several small, pore-like gill openings. Also, lampreys do not have teeth as the swamp eel does.

Threat. Because the invasive swamp eel is a generalist predator, it could impact native fishes, amphibians, and invertebrates in the areas where it is invasive. They are known to prey upon a variety of aquatic species including frogs, turtle eggs, shrimp and other invertebrates.

The overall potential negative impacts of swamp to native species, aquatic habitats, and overall ecosystems in areas where they are invasive are yet to be defined.

SWAMP EEL STIR FRY
SERVES 4

INGREDIENTS

2 lbs	Swamp eel
½ cup	Carrots, shredded
½ lb	Green beans, thin
1 bunch	Green onions, cut long way
1 ea	Red onion, sliced
¼ cup	Water
2 tbsp	Brown sugar
2 tbsp	Soy sauce
4 tbsp	Sweet & sour sauce
2 tbsp	White wine
4 tbsp	Olive oil
2 cups	Rice, steamed
To Taste	Seasoning to taste

COOKING INSTRUCTIONS

» Cut eel in one inches pieces then wash well under cold water

» In a sauté or Wok, heat olive oil

» Sauté eel pieces on medium-high temperature until golden brown

» Add brown sugar and seasoning stir well for 2 minutes

» Add remaining ingredients, stir well

» Cover with top and simmer for 15 minutes, or until vegetables are to desired consistency

» Serve with rice

INVASIVE SPECIES RECIPE

BIGHEAD CARP AKA COPI

INVASIVE SPECIES PROFILE

Geography. The bighead carp is native to major Pacific waters in eastern Asia— from the Amur River of far Eastern Russia, South through most of China to the Pearl River and northern Vietnam..

It is invasive in over 20 states throughout the Mississippi River Valley.

Description. It is a large narrow fish with downward projecting eyes that is dark gray on its dorsal side and fades to white on its belly. It has darker-colored blotches on the sides. It has no scales on its head and a large mouth with no teeth, a protruding lower jaw, and eyes that are far forward and low on its head.

These fast-growing fish can reach up to 100 pounds and over 60 inches in length. Each female bighead carp can produce up to one million eggs in a single year.

Threat. Bighead carp feed on plankton, a primary food for many native fish, including walleye, yellow perch, and lake whitefish. They are gluttonous, consuming up to 40% of their body weight every day. This ravenous invasive carp easily out competes native species for space and food causing disruption to the ecosystem that affects aquatic species, waterfowl and others.

This carp populate near shore areas and large rivers and may reduce recreational and commercial fishing opportunities.

BIGHEAD CARP SLIDERS
SERVES 8

INGREDIENTS

4 lbs	Bighead carp fillets
2 ea	Tomatoes, sliced
2 ea	Avocados sliced
1 ea	Red onion, sliced
2 cups	Heart Romaine lettuce
½ cup	Ranch dressing
16 ea	Mini-buns of your choice,
To Taste	Hot sauce to taste
To Taste	Seasoning to taste

INVASIVE SPECIES RECIPE

COOKING INSTRUCTIONS

» Season to taste bighead carp fillets
» Grill or pan sauté carp until well done
» Remove bones by hand and place cooked fish onto one side buns
» Top with tomatoes, avocados, red onions, romaine lettuce
» Add ranch dressing and hot sauce
» Cover with the other half of the bun
» Serve warm

THIS RECIPE CAN BE USED WITH ANY TYPE OF INVASIVE CARP!

NOTES

RECIPES FOR INVASIVE SHELLFISH SPECIES
CRUSTACEANS ⚓ MOLLUSKS

RED CRAWFISH

INVASIVE SPECIES PROFILE

Geography. The red crawfish (or crayfish) is native to the Southern Mississippi River Basin and along the southern U.S. Gulf Coast. It has become invasive in over 30 other U.S. states.. It is believed they most likely spread to invasive states through aquaculture (primarily cultivating for fishing bait) and through the aquarium trade.

Description. The red swamp crawfish, also known as Louisiana crawfish or swamp crawfish, has elongated claws and head and has a triangular rostrum that tapers toward the tail with a bony exoskeleton. It has two long antennae, two pincer claws, and eight legs that extend from a multi-part carapace that goes from the head along the body to the tail. The head and carapace are dark red, and the underside of the tail has a thick black stripe.

Threat. In non-native habitats, the red crawfish tends to overeat aquatic vegetation which causes harm to native aquatic species who depend on that vegetation for food, shelter, and spawning.

Red crawfish also cause an increase in cyanobacteria which is especially harmful because it reduces the amount of oxygen in the water which can be detrimental to native species in the affected waters.

Red crawfish also burrow which can cause infrastructure damage to dams, levees, and irrigation systems.

CAJUN STYLE BOILED RED CRAWFISH
SERVES 2

INGREDIENTS

6 lbs	Whole red crawfish washed,
3 gal	Water
4 ea	Onions, cut in wedges
5 ea	Lemons, cut in quarters
4 ea	Red potatoes, small
2 ea	Cobs of corn, cut in halves
6 oz	Mushrooms, whole
4 ea	Garlic cloves, whole
To Taste	Salt to taste
To Taste	Cayenne (red) pepper to taste

COOKING INSTRUCTIONS

- In a stock pot, boil water
- Add onions, garlic, lemons, red potatoes, salt, and red pepper
- Boil for 10 minutes, stirring as needed
- Add corn and mushroom
- Boil for 5 minutes, stirring as needed
- Add live crawfish to the pot
- Simmer for 15 minutes, stirring as needed
- Turn off the fire and let it sit in a hot pot for 15 minutes
- Pluck the tails! Suck the heads!
- Peel the meat out and enjoy your Cajun-style crawfish boil

In the state of Louisiana, Crawfish boils are a huge tradition, often with large groups of family and friends. Some of the things Louisianians add to their boil pot include: sausage, asparagus, hot dogs for the kids, halved oranges or lemons or limes, whole artichokes, whole green beans, broccoli, cauliflower, Brussels sprouts, whole eggs boiled and peeled, and garlic cloves. The most important thing at a "Louisiana Boil"? That's easy! Enjoy the food and have a great time!

Laissez les bons temps rouler: Let the good times roll!

INVASIVE SPECIES RECIPE

EUROPEAN GREEN CRAB

INVASIVE SPECIES PROFILE

Geography. The European green crab, also known as the shore crab, is native to Africa and Western Europe. They arrived in North America by hitching a ride in the ballast water of merchant ships during the 1800s.

It is invasive along the northeast Atlantic coast in the United States as well as in the Pacific coasts of Alaska, Washington, Oregon, and California

Description. The European green crab is not always green. For starters, juvenile green crabs can change color to match their environment each time they molt. They come in all colors of the rainbow and can be multi-hued.

Their most distinguishing feature is the "five points" on each side of the face. They have one pair of pincer claws, two forward-body claws, and two pairs of walking legs, one longer than the others. Another distinguishing feature of the green crab is five short spines behind each eye along the carapace.

Threat. This species presents a particular challenge in the northwest and, for the first time, has been identified in Alaska. It feeds on small fish, including salmon smolt, juvenile razor clams, juvenile oysters, and native crab species. But it also eats native vegetation that is critical to the aquatic ecosystem.

GREEN CRAB BISQUE
SERVES 4

INGREDIENTS

2 doz	Green crabs, whole, alive
¼ cup	Brandy liquor
2 cups	Sweet white wine
¼ cup	Tomato puree
4 cups	Water
4 oz	Butter, unsalted
1 oz	Regular white flour
1 oz	Vegetable oil
To Taste	Seasoning to taste

COOKING INSTRUCTIONS

» Preheat oven to 350° F.

» Wash green crabs thoroughly and slightly crush them by hand in a bowl

» Place crushed crabs in a baking pan and bake for 15 minutes

» Heat vegetable oil in a pan on medium heat, add flour, and constantly stir until you have a light, brown roux

» Remove from heat, set aside

» When crabs are done, pour brandy over crabs, then pour in a soup pot, add sweet white wine, water, and tomato puree and simmer for 20 minutes while gently stirring

» Strain juice back into the soup pot and bring to a low boil; add roux slowly to the soup pot and mix well until the consistency is of a bisque and simmer for 5 minutes

» Melt unsalted butter into bisque with a slow stir

» Season to taste and serve hot with your favorite bread or crackers

BLACK TIGER SHRIMP

INVASIVE SPECIES PROFILE

Geography. The black tiger shrimp is native to Asia and is also known as the Giant Tiger Prawn. It is invasive in the United States along the Gulf Coast and the southeastern Atlantic coast from Texas around the Florida peninsula to North Carolina.

Description. This aggressive shrimp can grow to 12 inches in length and weigh up to a full pound. It appears similar to other shrimp but has black stripes along its body and tail. It can also have a black body with orange stripes on its back.

Threat. The black tiger shrimp preys on smaller and weaker native shrimp species in waters where it is invasive. It is also known to eat oysters.

Black tiger shrimp are known to carry up to 16 different diseases which they can easily pass to native aquatic species which even further endangers them when these invasive shrimp are present.

Due to the traits stated above, the black tiger shrimp is a huge risk to the commercial shrimp and oyster industries along the Gulf States and other invaded areas.

There is a concerted effort in many coastal states to stop the invasive black tiger shrimp from reproducing and spreading further.

SHRIMP IN LEMON CREAM SAUCE
SERVES 2

INGREDIENTS

12 ea	Black tiger shrimp, peeled and cleaned
2 oz	Butter, unsalted
2 tbsp	Olive oil
1 tbsp	Chopped garlic
4 tbsp	White wine
2 tbsp	Lemon juice
½ cup	Heavy cream
To Taste	Seasoning to taste

INVASIVE SPECIES RECIPE

COOKING INSTRUCTIONS

» Season shrimp to taste
» In a skillet, combine butter and olive and melt the solution until hot
» Sauté shrimp for 1 to 2 minutes on each side until cooked
» Add garlic and sauté for 20-30 seconds
» Remove shrimp from the skillet
» Add white wine and lemon juice into the skillet
» Reduce for 2 minutes
» Add heavy cream and reduce for 2 more minutes
» Add cooked shrimp into the sauce
» Simmer for 1 minute and serve hot

GOLDEN CLAM

INVASIVE SPECIES PROFILE

Geography. The golden clam is native to Southern and Eastern Asia. Though it was first introduced in Washington, the species has invaded states to the East Coast and thrives in the Mississippi River Basin. It is now invasive in the United States in nearly all contiguous states as well as in Puerto Rico and Hawaii.

It is believed that it was originally brought to the U.S. as a food source for the immigrating Chinese population in the early 1900s. It is also possible that they were stowaways with imported Giant Pacific Oysters which also originate in Asia.

Description. The golden clam is a small light-colored bivalve whose shell is marked by distinct, concentric furrows and teeth with very fine serrations at the back. There are darker-colored and lighter-colored morphs of this species. The light-colored shell has a yellow-green to light brown color, while the darker morph is dark olive to black. Yellow and brown shell morphs have also been found in some areas.

Threat. Like all invasive species, this clam competes with native species for resources. It has been discovered that the species impacts the growth of native mussels, for example.

Because of bio-fouling, the clams can also cause problems in irrigation canals and pipes and drinking water supplies.

GOLDEN CLAM CHOWDER
SERVES 6

INGREDIENTS

10 ea	Golden clams, large, alive
2 tbsp	Olive oil
1 tbsp	Garlic, minced
2 tbsp	Regular white flour
¼ cup	White wine
2 tbsp	Lemon juice
1 cup	Canned clam juice
1 cup	Chicken stock
1 cup	Heavy cream
1 ea	Onion, medium, diced
1 ea	Celery stalk, diced
1 ea	Carrots, medium, diced
2 ea	Red bell peppers, diced
To Taste	Seasoning to taste

INVASIVE SPECIES RECIPE

COOKING INSTRUCTIONS

» In a stock pot, heat olive oil with garlic (do not brown garlic)
» Add fresh, live golden clams and cover the pot
» Steam clams on the stove until they open and release natural juices
» Remove clams from the pot
» Remove meat from shells and chop meat into small pieces
» Sprinkle flour evenly into the stock pot mixture and stir well
» Add chopped clam meat, onions, celery, carrots, bell pepper, clam juice, white wine, lemon juice, and chicken stock
» Simmer for 20 minutes
» Add cream and simmer for 15 minutes or until desired consistency
» Season to taste and serve hot

ZEBRA MUSSEL

INVASIVE SPECIES PROFILE

Geography. The zebra mussel is native to the Black Sea, the Caspian Sea, and the Azov Sea.

They were accidentally introduced to America in the Great Lakes in 1988 through the discharged ballast water of a ship that originated in the Caspian Sea.

They have spread rapidly throughout the Great Lakes region and into the large rivers of the eastern Mississippi drainage. They have also been found in Texas, Colorado, Utah, Nevada, and California.

Description. The zebra mussel is a small shellfish that has a striped pattern on its shell and a flat bottom surface. The color patterns vary so greatly that sometimes there is no pattern, only a dark or light-colored shell. Their coloring ranges from yellow and white to various shades of brown.

Threat. Zebra mussels negatively impact ecosystems by filtering out algae that native species need for food. They also attach to and incapacitate native mussel species.

Zebra mussels are also known to encrust equipment such as boat motors and hulls resulting in costly cleaning and repair.

Millions of dollars are spent removing zebra mussels from clogged water intakes of power plants, water filtration systems, and irrigation systems.

STUFFED ZEBRA MUSSELS
SERVES 4

INGREDIENTS

2 doz	Zebra mussels, large-size
¼ cup	White wine
4	Shallots, chopped
2 ea	Garlic cloves, minced
½ cup	Parmesan cheese,
½ cup	grated Breadcrumbs
½ cup	Butter, unsalted, melted
To Taste	Seasoning to taste

INVASIVE SPECIES RECIPE

COOKING INSTRUCTIONS

» Preheat oven to 350° F.

» Wash Zebra mussels well

» In a stock pot, add white wine, shallots, and garlic

» Bring to a boil, then add zebra mussels then boil and stir well for 5 minutes

» Separate zebra mussels from the liquid and put the liquid in a separate bowl with garlic and shallots

» Add melted butter to juice and season to taste, then stir well

» In a separate bowl, mix Parmesan and breadcrumbs with the liquid garlic shallots mixture

» Place mussel on bread toast and top with breadcrumb mixture

» Bake Zebra mussel toast at 350° F for 5 minutes or until golden brown

» Serve hot with favorite side dishes

APPLE SNAIL

INVASIVE SPECIES PROFILE

Geography. The apple snail is native to South America and was introduced to the United States through the aquarium trade. It is very common in many freshwater aquariums. It is currently considered invasive in over 10 U.S. states along the coastline of the Gulf of Mexico and the Atlantic.

Description. Also known as the Island Apple Snail, it is most easily identified by its globular, spiraled shell. Apple snails can grow up to 6 inches in length.

Most apple snails have spiral shells that vary in colors, including yellow, black, brown, and tan. They often have brown bands that follow the spiral of the shell.

Apple snail eggs are bright reddish-pink and are laid, often on plants, in groups of 200 - 600. Apple snails lay their eggs above the water level and are easy to identify in the wild.

Threat. Apple snails feast on aquatic vegetation and other snail species. Their feeding can radically modify nutrients in an aquatic ecosystem.

These freshwater snails are amphibious and can survive seasonally in terrestrial and aquatic environments, including lakes, ponds, and wetlands.

Check your local wildlife laws before harvesting apple snails or their eggs. Some states have strict regulations about harvest of these invasive crustaceans.

APPLE SNAIL PROVENÇALE
SERVES 4

INGREDIENTS

1 doz	Fresh apple snails, alive
2 cups	Rock salt
3 qt	Water
2 qt	Chicken stock
1 cup	Tomato sauce
4 oz	Butter, unsalted
2 tbsp	Italian breadcrumbs
1 tbsp	Garlic, minced
¼ cup	Parmesan cheese grated
To Taste	Seasoning to taste

COOKING INSTRUCTIONS

- Put live snails and rock salt in a container
- Cure live snails for 3 hours in salt
- Remove snails from salt
- Wash thoroughly in warm running water
- In a stock pot, boil snails in water for 30-minute
- Remove snails from the heat
- While warm, remove snail meat from the shell with a small fork
- Remove the digestive offal from the muscle
- In a stock pot, add chicken stock, onion, and garlic, then bring to a boil for 5 minutes
- Reduce heat and simmer apple snail muscle for 45 minutes until tender.
- Remove cooked snail muscles from broth and chop each one into quarters
- In a sauté pan, heat butter on medium heat until light brown
- Add tomato sauce, garlic, and cooked Apple snails to the pan and mix well
- Simmer for 5 minutes
- Add bread crumble and Parmesan cheese to the mixture in the pan
- Mix well and simmer for 3 minutes
- Stir well and season to taste
- Serve over toasted bread of choice

INVASIVE SPECIES RECIPE

NOTES

RECIPES FOR INVASIVE MAMMAL SPECIES

FERAL SWINE (WILD BOAR)

INVASIVE SPECIES PROFILE

Geography. Feral Swine is a population of multiple wild boar species, all of which originated in Eurasia and were brought to America by European settlers and explorers who came from Spain. They were brought to America as a source of food.

Feral Swine, sometimes called feral hogs, feral pigs, or wild boar, are invasive in most North American U.S. states.

Description. Feral Swine are usually brown to black with grizzled guard hairs and a short hair mane that runs from the neck to the tail. They have a short straight tufted tails, and hair covers their ears. They have rounded body contours, short legs, and cloven hooves with four toes, two of which are large dewclaws.

Threat. The population of these hogs now reaches 38 states, with more than 5 million animals.

Louisiana Department of Wildlife and Fisheries officials estimate it would take harvesting 75% of the population to contain it and keep it at manageable levels.

These wild pigs are extremely destructive, causing over $1 Billion annually in damage. They not only eat vegetation which is important to native species in an invaded ecosystem but also trample undisturbed and disturbed lands in a harmful manner.

SWEET BERRY WILD BOAR
SERVES 8

INGREDIENTS

2 lbs	Wild boar backstrap, cut in 1-inch cubes
4 oz	Butter, unsalted
1 pt	Fresh blackberries *
4 oz	Blackberry Jam
1 cup	Onion, chopped
2 tbsp	Garlic, minced
2 tbsp	Flour, regular
½ cup	Red wine
1 cup	Beef broth
To Taste	Seasoning to taste

COOKING INSTRUCTIONS

- In a stock pot, melt butter until brown and add wild boar meat
- Stir until light brown; add onions and garlic, and stir for 3 minutes
- Add flour, stir until flour is dissolved, add red wine and beef broth, and stir well
- Bring to a simmer, add blackberry jam, and season to taste
- Stir well and simmer for 35 minutes or until meat is fully cooked
- Serve garnished with fresh blackberries

* Double up the Can't Beat 'Em, Eat 'Em and use Invasive Himalayan Blackberries!

FOX SQUIRREL

INVASIVE SPECIES PROFILE

Geography. The fox squirrel is native to the eastern United States, excluding the New England area. They have become invasive in other areas of the United States including California, Idaho, Montana, Oregon, Washington, Wyoming, and possibly others..

Description. The fox squirrel is the largest of the four types of squirrels. Despite that, they are the more difficult species to find in the wild.. There are seven subspecies of fox squirrel, and almost all of them are nearly twice the size of the common gray squirrel. The size and sport of finding them make this a popular animal among hunters.

They have a long furry tail with fur color that varies from pale gray to black, with the most common being a reddish-brown color. They have white feet, and some have white bellies.

Some subspecies of fox squirrel have reddish fur with ends that are a lighter color giving them a "frosted" look.

Threat. These larger invasive squirrels are known to damage property and agricultural crops. They are also out competing native squirrels for food and nesting space in areas where they are invasive. They can be found in urban areas such as parks and residential neighborhoods as well as in the wild.

FOX SQUIRREL RAVIGOTE
SERVES 4

INGREDIENTS

8 ea	Fox squirrel hindquarters
1 qt	Beef stock
1 cup	Red wine
½ cup	Tomato puree
1 tbsp	Red wine vinegar
½ cup	Dill pickle, chopped
2 tbsp	Cane sugar
To Taste	Seasoning to taste

COOKING INSTRUCTIONS

- Wash fox squirrel hind quarters and season to taste
- In a stew pot, pour beef stock, red wine, tomato puree, and vinegar
- Bring to a boil
- Put seasoned fox squirrel hind quarters into stock
- Add chopped pickle and sugar
- Bring to a boil
- Simmer for 40 minutes or until fully cooked
- Serve with baked potatoes

NUTRIA

INVASIVE SPECIES PROFILE

Geography. The Nutria is native to South America in Argentina, Bolivia, Brazil, Chile, Paraguay, and Uruguay. They are currently considered invasive in over 30 U.S. states.

Description. Nutria is smaller than a beaver but larger than a muskrat. They have a round, slightly-haired tails. Their forelegs seem small compared to their body size.

Their forepaws have four clawed toes and a smaller fifth toe without a claw. Their hind legs are larger than the front legs, making their backs hunched. It also places their fore-body close to the ground when they walk.

The hind paws have four clawed, webbed toes and a fifth toe that is not webbed.

Nutria are usually dark brown but have also been observed in lighter shades of brown and an albino variation.

They have a pyramid-shaped head with a dark, arrowhead-shaped wedge whose point extends away from the body toward the nose.

Threat. Each Nutria consumes a quarter of its body weight daily. They eat plants and root systems literally destroying invaded ecosystems.

In addition, Nutria burrow into the ground which is damaging to banks and levees as well as earth that supports various infrastructure such as piers, docks, foundations, streams, lakes, rivers, roads, dams, and more.

RAGONDIN (NUTRIA) CROCK POT
SERVES 8 - 10

HEART HEALTHY

INVASIVE SPECIES RECIPE

INGREDIENTS

4 lbs	Ragondin hind quarters
1 lb	Carrots, diced
1 lb	Green cabbage, sliced
1 lb	Red petite potatoes
1 ea	Onion, medium, chopped
4 ea	Garlic cloves, minced
2 ea	Whole bay leaves
1 cup	Chicken broth, low-sodium
To Taste	Seasoning to taste

COOKING INSTRUCTIONS

» Season hind quarters to taste
» Grill hind quarters until golden brown
» Cut meat into desired bite size and put aside
» In a crock pot, put carrots, cabbage, potatoes, onion, garlic, bay leaves, chicken broth, grilled meat pieces, and seasoning to taste.
» Cook on medium heat for 30 minutes
» Serve as is or over rice

EUROPEAN RABBIT

INVASIVE SPECIES PROFILE

Geography. The European rabbit is native to southern Europe and northern Africa. As invasive as European rabbits are in the United States and other countries, especially Australia, they are rapidly becoming an endangered species in their native habitats.

Description. The European rabbit has a coat that is primarily shades of gray with black, brown (and sometimes red) sprinkled throughout their bodies. The underside of their bodies is a paler shade of gray, and the bottom of their tails is white. Darker-colored coats are also standard in some areas.

European rabbits have two pairs of upper incisor teeth, with the second smaller found behind the first, which makes it easier for them to nibble grass, shoots, leaves, and stems.

Threat. European rabbits are aggressive foragers who are a huge threat to biodiversity when they become established in non-native areas.

Their quick reproduction allows them to establish a territory where they consume a variety of food. They out compete native species for space and food. They are capable of completely deleting food sources in invaded areas, including agricultural crops.

They are considered an agricultural pest and an ecological threat in all invaded areas. Millions of dollars are spent annually to control, confine, or eliminate them from invaded areas.

EUROPEAN RABBIT WITH MUSHROOMS
SERVES 4

INGREDIENTS

1 ea	European rabbit cut into 8 pieces
¼ cup	Vegetable oil
2 cups	Mushrooms of choice, sliced
2 tbsp	Flour regular
½ cup	Red wine
2 cups	Chicken stock
½ cup	Onion, chopped
3 ea	Garlic cloves
¼ cup	Heavy cream
To Taste	Seasoning to taste

INVASIVE SPECIES RECIPE

COOKING INSTRUCTIONS

- In a stew pot, heat oil over medium-high heat
- Add rabbit pieces and brown by stirring and flipping
- Add onion and garlic and continue stirring for 1 minute
- Add flour and mix well until flour dissolves
- Add mushrooms, wine, and chicken stock, then stir well
- Bring to a boil
- Simmer for 30 minutes, gently stirring every 10 minutes until fully cooked
- Add heavy cream and simmer for 5 minutes
- Season to taste
- Serve hot

AXIS (SPOTTED) DEER

INVASIVE SPECIES PROFILE

Geography. The spotted deer is native to India, Nepal, and Sri Lanka and was brought to the U.S. in the 1930s as a game animal. They are now invasive in several U.S. states.

Description. Axis deer look like most deer but have an orange-colored coat with white spots, similar to a whitetail deer fawn. Mature males and females have white patches on their throats.

Male axis deer grow antlers as they mature. Male antlers have an average of 6 points per antler. Males are also known to "bugle" during mating season.

Threat. It occupies the same ecological niche as the whitetail deer and competes with the whitetail for food and space by drastically reducing native vegetation.

In addition, male axis deer are also known to damage or even kill native trees by rubbing and polishing their antlers on tree bark.

With increased resistance to native diseases, axis deer are not susceptible to the same population decreases resulting from local disease outbreaks as the whitetail. Because of the disease resistance, the axis deer populations could grow out of control.

If the axis population gets out of control, farmers are at risk of damage as herds forage cultivated fields or gardens.

AXIS DEER WITH CHERRY SAUCE
SERVES 8

INGREDIENTS

4 ea	Axis deer back strap
½ cup	Brown sugar
1 cup	Red wine
8 oz	Cherry preserves
4 oz	Butter, unsalted, melted
To Taste	Seasoning to taste

INVASIVE SPECIES RECIPE

COOKING INSTRUCTIONS

» Preheat oven to 350° F.
» Season back straps to taste
» Dust brown sugar on seasoned back strap
» Place back place strap in a roasting pan with butter
» Back for 10 minutes
» Flip back strap over and bake for another 5 minutes.
» Remove from oven and pour red wine mixed with cherry preserves over roasted strap
» Return to oven and bake for another 10 minutes or until fully cooked
» Slice the cooked backstraps and top with red wine cherry sauce
» Serve hot

FERAL GOAT

INVASIVE SPECIES PROFILE

Geography. Goats were domesticated in Iran over 10,000 years ago, but the feral goats in the United States are believed to be native to Asia and were brought here by explorers as a source of food and drink. Many were released into the wild by those same explorers and others were marooned here due to shipwrecks. They are currently invasive in several U.S. states.

Description. These typical-looking goats are usually black to various shades of brown and can be single- or multi-colored. A typical color pattern is a darker front with a lighter backside. Horns are dimorphic and spiral toward the back. Most feral goat species have a long, flat tail and long, pointed ears. Some feral goats may also have white or red coloring along with the other colors.

Threat. It has been determined by authorities that feral goats consumer and trample native plant species to such a degree that native vegetation ecosystem are heavily damaged if not completely destroyed.

Feral goats also carry diseases which are easily spread to native species causing illness and death..

All of these issues are exacerbated since these invasive goat species is very mobile and can cover a large area of land as needed. When the habitat gets over-grazed or otherwise undesirable, they simply move to new territory.

FERAL GOAT DIJON
SERVES 6

INGREDIENTS

1 ea	Feral goat hind quarter
½ cup	Dijon mustard
1 cup	Olive oil
2 cups	Red wine
4 oz	Butter, unsalted, melted
To Taste	Seasoning to taste

COOKING INSTRUCTIONS

» Preheat oven to 350° F.
» Season to taste the leg of goat
» Evenly coat with Dijon mustard and place leg into baking pan
» Mix olive oil with melted butter, then pour over the leg of the goat
» Bake at 350 F. for 20 minutes flip the leg 2 to 3 times while baking
» Pour red wine over goat leg
» Cover leg with foil and bake for 20 more minutes or until fully cooked
» Slice meat off bones and place on serving dish; drizzle with sauce from baking pan
» Serve hot with our favorite side dish

INVASIVE SPECIES RECIPE

NOTES

RECIPES FOR INVASIVE AVIAN SPECIES
DUCKS ⚊ GEESE ⚊ OTHER BIRDS

MUSCOVY DUCK

INVASIVE SPECIES PROFILE

Geography. The Muscovy duck is native to South America, Central America, Mexico, and three counties in southern Texas.

They have spread to non-native areas due to overpopulation and reduction of migration and native habitats. They are often introduced to non-native areas as pets released into the wild. Muscovy ducks are currently invasive in several U.S. states including Louisiana, Florida, New York, and parts of Texas.

Description. Muscovy ducks are black with distinct patches of white on their wings or white with black patches on their wings. Iridescent blue, green, or violet can sometimes be found on their wings and tail feathers. Their face is red or black with a black bill marked with pale pink spots. Their legs and feet are black.

Threat. If a non-native population of Muscovy ducks goes unchecked, they can grow rapidly to a state of overpopulation.

Larger than most ducks, the females weigh up to ten pounds, and the males are two to five pounds heavier.

While it isn't thought that these ducks pose any specific harm to humans, it is considered by many as a nuisance and considered by some U.S. states as invasive.

MUSCOVY DUCK À L'ORANGE
SERVES 4

INGREDIENTS

1 ea	Muscovy duck, cleaned
4 oz	Butter, unsalted
1 cup	Orange juice
1 bunch	Green onions, cut long way
½ cup	Red wine
2 oz	Light brown sugar
8 ea	Orange slices, peeled
To Taste	Seasoning to taste

INVASIVE SPECIES RECIPE

COOKING INSTRUCTIONS

» Preheat oven to 350° F.
» Dry the cleaned Muscovy duck with paper towels
» Coat the duck with seasoning to taste and place the duck in a roasting pan
» Pour melted butter over the duck
» Bake for 20 minutes
» Remove from oven and sprinkle light brown sugar over duck
» Continue baking for 10 minutes
» Remove from oven and add red wine and orange juice to the pan
» Cover with aluminum foil, and bake for 30 minutes or until fully cooked
» Remove from oven and cut duck into quarters
» Place a quarter on the serving dish and top with orange sauce
» Garnish with orange slices and serve hot

ROCK DOVE (COMMON PIGEON)

INVASIVE SPECIES PROFILE

Geography. The Rock dove, commonly called a pigeon, is native to Europe and came to America with the first settlers at Plymouth as messenger birds and as a source of food.

They are currently present in every U.S. state and territory and in nearly every major city around the world. Everywhere they are present, they are considered either a nuisance or invasive avian species.

Description. Rock doves are commonly seen with gray to blue bodies, iridescent throat feathers, black tips or bands on the wing tips, and black bands on the tip of the tail. They regularly have extreme variations in color, and the banding pattern on the wings can be one band, two bands, or no bands at all.

Threat. Pigeon droppings accelerate the deterioration of the exterior of buildings, increase building maintenance costs, and spread diseases.

Around grain handling facilities, pigeons consume and contaminate large quantities of food destined for human or livestock consumption.

Pigeons around airports can also threaten human safety because of potential bird-aircraft collisions and are considered a medium-priority hazard to jet aircraft by the U. S. Air Force.

ROCK DOVE (PIGEON) STEW
SERVES 4

INGREDIENTS

4 ea	Pigeon
4 tbsp	Vegetable oil
2 tbsp.	Flour, regular
1 cup	Red wine
1 qt	Chicken stock
¼ cup	Heavy cream
To Taste	Seasoning to taste

COOKING INSTRUCTIONS

» Add vegetable oil to stew pot and heat on medium heat

» When the oil is hot, put pigeon quarters in a stew pot and stir until all parts are golden brown

» Add flour and stir well until flour disappears

» Add red wine and chicken stock

» Simmer for 20 minutes or until fully cooked

» Add cream and simmer for 5 more minutes

» Season to taste

» Serve hot

SNOW GOOSE

INVASIVE SPECIES PROFILE

Geography. The snow goose is native to North America and both the arctic and subarctic regions of Russia.

The snow goose population has increased from an estimated 800,000 in the 1950s to over 6 million today. They are invasive in more than 25 continental U.S. states.

They have become invasive in non-native areas due to over population and natural seasonal migration.

Description. The snow goose appears in two phases: the "snow" phase and the "blue" phase. The "snow" phase is a snowy white body with black wing tips. They have red feet and legs with a pink bill and a black patch of skin surrounding the base of the bill. In the "blue" phase, it has the same feet, legs, bill, skin patch, and wing tips but has blue/gray body with a white neck, underbelly, and head.

Threat. Aggressive eaters, snow geese pull plants up by the roots and eat the whole plant. They also eat grains and fruits. In some areas, farmers view this species as a pest.

Despite the high populations of snow geese, some Wildlife and Fisheries agencies have strict hunting seasons for snow geese. Check your local laws before harvesting this species.

ONE POT GLAZED SNOW GOOSE
SERVES 4

INGREDIENTS

4 ea	Snow goose breast
2 tbsp	Olive oil
¼ cup	Onion, chopped
1 tbsp	Garlic, minced
2 tbsp	Sugar
¼ cup	Red wine
1 tbsp	Red wine vinegar
2 tbsp	Lemon juice
4 tbs	Orange juice
To Taste	Seasoning to taste

COOKING INSTRUCTIONS

» Prepare mashed potatoes or steamed rice, set aside

» Tenderize goose breasts with light pounding and season breasts to taste

» Coat seasoned breast evenly with sugar

» Add olive oil in a deep skillet or sauté pan on medium-high heat

» Sauté seasoned goose breasts, approximately 2 minutes on each side

» Remove breasts from pan and set aside

» Add onions and garlic to the pan and sauté for approximately 2 minutes

» Add browned breasts back into the pan with sautéed garlic and onions

» Add lemon juice, orange juice, red wine, and vinegar and simmer for 10 minutes or until breasts are fully cooked

» Serve breast over mashed potatoes or rice, then top with sauce

CANADA GOOSE

INVASIVE SPECIES PROFILE

Geography. The Canada goose is native to Canada, the northern United States (including Alaska), and several other areas in the Northern Hemisphere. They become invasive when they do not leave migration areas.

These geese stay in migration areas due to overpopulation and/or human interference (infrastructure and other disturbances) in native nesting areas. They are currently invasive in all of or at least part of every U.S. state.

Description. The Canada goose has a black head and crown and a long black neck. Its cheeks are covered with white patches. The body feathers are grayish brown or tan, which darkens into the tail feathers. They have a white underbelly and black feet and legs.

Threat. It is difficult to believe, but over-hunting a little over 100 years ago drove Canadian geese close to extinction. Today, the opposite problem exists with the overpopulation of this invasive species.

They endanger public health by soiling lakes, stripping farmers' fields, and damaging equipment such as airplanes, farm equipment, and industrial equipment.

Verify your local laws regarding hunting and harvesting the Canada goose.

CANADA GOOSE PARMIGIANA
SERVES 8

INGREDIENTS

4 ea	Canada goose breast, skinless
2 ea	Eggs, beaten
½ cup	Half & Half
1 cup	Breadcrumbs
2 tbsp	Olive oil
¼ cup	Mushrooms, sliced
½ cup	Onion, sliced
1 tbsp	Garlic, minced
1 cup	Marinara sauce
½ cup	Parmesan cheese, grated
½ cup	Mozzarella cheese, shredded
Serve 8	Cooked pasta of choice
To Taste	Seasoning to taste

INVASIVE SPECIES RECIPE

COOKING INSTRUCTIONS

- Preheat oven to 350° F.
- Pound the Canada goose breasts to the desired thickness
- Season the goose breasts to taste
- In a bowl mix eggs well and Half & Half
- Dip the seasoned breasts into mixture and coat evenly with bread crumbs
- Heat olive oil in skillet
- Sauté breaded goose breasts until golden brown
- When well-cooked and golden brown remove breasts from skillet and place into baking pan
- In hot skillet, sauté onions, mushrooms, and chopped garlic for 2 minutes than topped over breast.
- Top breasts with sauté
- Pour marinara sauce over breasts
- Top the breasts with Parmesan and Mozzarella cheese
- Bake at 350° F for 10 minutes or until fully cooked.
- Serve with preferred cooked pasta

NOTES

RECIPES FOR INVASIVE REPTILE AND AMPHIBIAN SPECIES

GREEN IGUANA

INVASIVE SPECIES PROFILE

Geography. The green iguana is native to southern Mexico through Central America to Ecuador and Brazil. Iguanas were introduced to the U.S. in the Florida Keys in the late 1800s as stowaways on ships delivering fruit from South America. It is primarily invasive due to releases into the wild by pet owners.

Description. The green iguana is one of the largest lizards in the United States and is colored in a range from brown to gray to black to varying shades of green. They are sometimes even colored an orange hue when they are mating. They have a crest of large spines along the back and tail with a large dewlap under the chin. Adult iguana often has black bands on their sides and tails.

Threat. Green iguanas have become especially invasive in South Florida, Hawaii, Texas, and Puerto Rico. They can be destructive in non-native ecosystems due to rapid breeding and appetites for expensive ornamental yard plants. Iguanas are attracted to trees with foliage or flowers, fruits, and vegetables. By digging burrows that cause erosion, this giant lizard can wreak havoc on infrastructures like sidewalks, foundations, and seawalls.

FRIED GREEN IGUANA TACOS
SERVES 4

INGREDIENTS

1 ea	Iguana hind quarter
2 cups	Corn meal flour
2 ea	Tomatoes*, diced
½ cup	Shredded cheese*
½ cup	Sour cream*
2 ea	Avocados*, sliced
¼ cup	Salsa of choice*
1 cup	Chopped lettuce*
8 ea	Taco shells or soft tortillas
To Taste	Seasoning to taste

For Toppings

INVASIVE SPECIES RECIPE

COOKING INSTRUCTIONS

» Wash Iguana hind quarters thoroughly and let dry on a paper towel

» Add seasoning to taste to cornmeal and mix well, then coat the hind quarter with seasoned cornmeal flour

» Using tongs, place the hind quarter into fryer for 20 minutes or until fully cooked

» Remove iguana from the oil and let it drip on a paper towel to drain grease

» Remove bone from meat and cut meat into small taco-size pieces

» Place meat in taco shells

» Garnish with toppings

» Serve hot

BURMESE PYTHON

INVASIVE SPECIES PROFILE

Geography. The Burmese python is native to India, lower China, the Malay Peninsula, and some islands in the East Indies.

It was introduced to America in the early 1980s through the exotic pet trade and is one of the largest snakes in the world. The first nest was discovered in the Florida Everglades in 2006.

They have become invasive in non-native areas due to over population and natural seasonal migration.

Description. The BURMESE PYTHON is tan with dark blotches along the back and sides that have been compared to puzzle pieces or the spots on a giraffe. They have a pyramid-shaped head with a dark, arrowhead-shaped wedge whose point extends away from the body toward the nose.

Threat. It is estimated that over ten thousand of these snakes are in the Everglades in Florida, eating native animals and causing significant ecosystem damage.

A single female Burmese python can lay clutches of up to 100 eggs per reproductive event.

Burmese pythons have few natural predators and will eat anything they can fit in their mouth. This makes them incredibly threatening to a non-native habitat.

Ironically, the species has been dramatically reduced in its native southeast Asia to the point of becoming endangered.

GOURMET PYTHON BURGERS
SERVES 4

INGREDIENTS

2 lbs	Python meat, boneless and skinless
4 qt	Water
4 tbs	Shallots, chopped finely
¼ cup	Cilantro, chopped finely
2 tbsp	Garlic, minced
1 ea	Egg, beaten
½ cup	Mayonnaise
¼ cup	Breadcrumbs
2 tbsp	Hot sauce
To Taste	Seasoning to taste

COOKING INSTRUCTIONS

» Boil water in stock pot

» Add python meat and simmer for 40 minutes

» Strain python meat and dry on a paper towel

» Add cooked python to a food processor and run for several seconds

» In a mixing bowl add chopped python meat with egg, shallots, cilantro, garlic, hot sauce, mayonnaise and breadcrumbs and season to taste

» Mix well.

» Cool texture overnight in the refrigerator

» The following day:

» Form patties in the desired size and bake at 350° F. or cook in pan until fully cooked

» Served as python burgers with bun and garnishments of choice

INVASIVE SPECIES RECIPE

RED-EARED SLIDER TURTLE

INVASIVE SPECIES PROFILE

Geography. The red-eared slider turtle is native to the Mississippi River drainage area in the southern United States but has become invasive in other parts of the country, primarily due to the pet trade industry.

Release of red-eared sliders has been happening since the 1930s and reached its peak during the late 1980s and 1990s as a surge in the sell of these turtles in the pet trade coincided with the skyrocketing popularity of four very famous celebrity turtles in cartoons, comic books, and movies.

Description. The red-eared slider turtle is a medium-sized turtle with olive or brown skin and a carapace. The carapace often appears greener in color.

The carapace's underside along the body's sides is usually yellow with large dark spots or patches.

It has yellow stripes or spots along the head and neck and a distinguishing red line on each side of its head. The colors, especially of the carapace, are brighter in juveniles.

Threat. The red-eared slider turtle plays a vital role as predator and prey in its native range. When they are introduced to non-native ecosystems, they become aggressive and bold. These turtles compete heavily for food and space with native turtles when they are out of their native environment.

RED-EARED SLIDER TURTLE SOUP
SERVES 8

INGREDIENTS

2 lbs	Snapping turtle meat
2 qt	Beef broth
1 cup	Tomato puree
½ cup	Onion, diced
½ cup	Celery, diced
½ cup	Carrot, diced
2 tbsp	Garlic, minced
½ cup	Sherry wine
1 oz	Vegetable oil
1 oz	Flour, regular
To Taste	Seasoning to taste

INVASIVE SPECIES RECIPE

COOKING INSTRUCTIONS

- Fill a stock pot ½ fill with water
- Add turtle meat and gently boil for 20 minutes
- Heat vegetable oil in a skillet on medium heat
- Add flour
- STIR CONSTANTLY until mixture is a rich brown color, being careful to not overcook (burn) it
- Remove from heat, set aside
- Strain turtle meat and chop into bite-size pieces
- In a separate pot, add beef broth, sherry wine, tomato puree, onion, celery, carrot, garlic, and chopped turtle meat and stir well
- Bring to a boil, stirring occasionally
- Simmer for 15 minutes
- Add roux and mix well
- Simmer for another 20 minutes or until desired consistency
- Season to taste
- Serve with your favorite bread or crackers

AMERICAN BULLFROG

INVASIVE SPECIES PROFILE

Geography. The American bullfrog called a bullfrog in the United States and Canada, is native to the Central and Southeastern United States but invasive in most other states. They are particularly causing issues in the American west.

Description. The American bullfrog is a giant frog that ranges in color from shades of brown to shades of green and sometimes has spots or blotches of a darker color on its back. It has fully webbed back feet.

American bullfrogs are usually found near lakes, ponds, rivers, bogs, marshes, swamps, streams, as well as drainage ditches, wading pools, and other smaller shallows that are of human origin. They especially like waters with aquatic vegetation which provides habitat for growth, reproduction, and cover from predators.

Threat. Because of the bullfrogs' size and ravenous appetites, they prey on many indigenous species.

They cause a significant impact on invaded ecosystems leading to the endangerment and extinction of other species.

With lifespans that range up to 10 years, these frogs can lay ten times the number of eggs at once than other species of frogs, so the populations can quickly and easily overwhelm the native frog species.

FRIED BULLFROG LEGS
SERVES 8

INGREDIENTS

16 ea	Bullfrog legs, skinned
1 cup	Milk
2 ea	Eggs, beaten
2 cups	Corn flour
4 tbsp	Lemon juice
4 oz	Butter
4 tbsp	Cilantro, chopped
2 tbsp	Garlic, chopped
To Taste	Seasoning to taste

INVASIVE SPECIES RECIPE

COOKING INSTRUCTIONS

- Wash frog legs and dry them on paper towels
- Season to taste
- Mix eggs and milk in a bowl (egg wash)
- Dip frog legs into the egg wash
- In a separate bowl, put corn flour and seasoning (to taste)
- Dip egg-washed frog legs into the flour mix, coating them completely
- Fry in oil (350 F) for 12 to 15 minutes or until fully cooked
- In a saucepan, lightly brown the butter over medium heat
- Add garlic and cilantro into hot butter for 5 seconds
- Add lemon juice and stir gently
- Top fried frog legs with lemon butter garlic cilantro sauce
- Serve hot

NOTES

RECIPES FOR INVASIVE PLANT SPECIES

KUDZU VINE

INVASIVE SPECIES PROFILE

Geography. The Kudzu vine is native to the Pacific Islands, China, Taiwan, Japan, and India.

The Kudzu was originally brought to two different World Fairs from Japan but were fully destroyed. Then, in the late 1800s, Kudzu seeds were sold in catalogs and imported as an ornamental vine.

By the mid 1900s, it had become a popular livestock forage vine and a soil erosion deterrent. This is when it began to spread all of the United States. It is currently considered invasive in over 30 states.

Description. Kudzu is a green, sometimes variegated, trifoliate-leaved, semi-woody, trailing, or climbing perennial vine. It is often confused with poison ivy but differs because kudzu stems are distinctively hairy, and the vines twine. Kudzu has individual purple flowers that grow in upright clusters and have a grape-like aroma. Some kudzu vines produce flowers that are redder than purple..

Threat. Because of its rapid growth (over one foot per day), Kudzu vine is known as *mile-a-minute* and *the vine that ate the South*. This creeping, climbing perennial vine terrorizes native plants, out-competing nearly all of them for space, including grasses and fully mature trees. This, in turn, has negative impacts on all native wildlife in the invaded ecosystem. It is considered one of the most invasive plants in America.

KUDZU PIE
SERVES 4

INGREDIENTS

2 cups	Kudzu leaves & blossoms
1 cup	Heavy cream
1 ea	Eggs, beaten
½ cup	Mozzarella cheese, grated
½ cup	Parmesan cheese, grated
½ cup	Ham, cooked, diced
2 ea	Pie crust, 9-inches
1 pinch	Nutmeg powder
To Taste	Seasoning to taste

COOKING INSTRUCTIONS

» Preheat oven to 350 F
» Wash well kudzu leaves and blossoms thoroughly under running water
» Boil in water for 2 minutes
» Drain water from kudzu, dry on paper towels, then chop into small pieces
» Mix well in a bowl the egg, cream, Parmesan, Mozzarella, ham, nutmeg, and other seasonings to taste
» Add seasoned chopped kudzu and other ingredients from the bowl into the pie crust
» Use the second pie crust as a topper on the pie
» Bake for 30 minutes at 350° F until pie crust is golden brown
» Serve hot

INVASIVE SPECIES RECIPE

HIMALAYAN BLACKBERRY

INVASIVE SPECIES PROFILE

Geography. The Himalayan or Armenian blackberry is an evergreen shrub native to Armenia and northern Iran.

It was introduced to the Unites States in Oregon by Luther Burbank in 1885 as a food crop. It is believed that the Himalayan blackberry spread to other states through normal seed dispersal and intentional transplants.

Description. The Himalayan blackberry has red/purple stems with three, four, or five green leaflets with thorns on the underside rib.

It blossoms in late spring, and early summer with white flowers and bears fruits aggregated drupelets that begin green, turn red, and finally dark purple or black when they mature.

Threat. While its berries are tasty, it is an aggressive, fast-spreading vine that can produce up to 13,000 seeds per square meter of occupation. In addition, the Himalayan blackberry has seed banks underground which can sprout and regrow, even in areas where it has been removed.

Himalayan blackberries thrive in sunny areas and can grow so thick that it shades out native plants, impedes the movement of large animals and livestock, and overwhelms and displaces native plants.

Today it represents a significant challenge to the American west, particularly the northwest. Some jurisdictions classify it as a noxious weed.

HIMALAYAN BLACKBERRY FLAMBÉ
SERVES 4

INGREDIENTS

2 cups	Himalaya blackberries
2 oz	Butter, unsalted
2 ea	Bananas, sliced
½ cup	Light brown sugar
2 oz	Dark rum
2 oz	Triple Sec (orange liqueur)
1 oz	Lemon juice
4 oz	Orange juice
4 scoops	Vanilla ice cream

INVASIVE SPECIES RECIPE

COOKING INSTRUCTIONS

- In a sauté pan, melt butter with light brown sugar on medium-high heat until a smooth texture
- Carefully pour Rum and Triple Sec into the mixture
- Light a flame in the pan for flambé
- Immediately after flambé dies down, add berries and banana
- Stir well
- Add lemon and orange juice, then stir for 2 minutes
- Serve over ice cream.

AUTUMN OLIVE/BERRY

INVASIVE SPECIES PROFILE

Geography. The Autumn olive (or berry) is native to Asia and was brought to America's New England in the 1830s for agricultural and horticultural use. It was specifically brought for use as a food source and to create natural habitat cover for native wildlife.

The Autumn olive is now considered invasive in over 35 U.S. states including every state east of the Mississippi River and all states bordering the river on the west side.

Description. The Autumn olive is a multi-branch, deciduous, shrubby tree with alternate leaves that vary in size. It produces thorns on the spur branches that bloom clusters of small yellow to white flowers before making single-seeded, round berries that are red to brown to pink in color. The silvery dotted underside of the leaves quickly identifies it.

Threat. After taking root, a single Autumn olive creates 200,000 seeds annually. It can spread rapidly and easily take over an ecosystem when it is outside its native habitat.

Autumn olive is a nitrogen fixer (increases nitrogen levels) and causes the local air, soil, and/or water to no longer be compatible with native species.

Autumn olive displaces native plants by shading them out and changing the chemistry of the soil. It is considered very dangerous to farmland and agricultural areas.

AUTUMN OLIVE JELLY
NUMEROUS SERVINGS

INGREDIENTS

5 lbs	Autumn Olive berries, ripe
½ cup	Cup water
3 lbs	Sugar
2 oz	Lemon juice
6 oz	Orange juice
3 tbsp	Vanilla extract

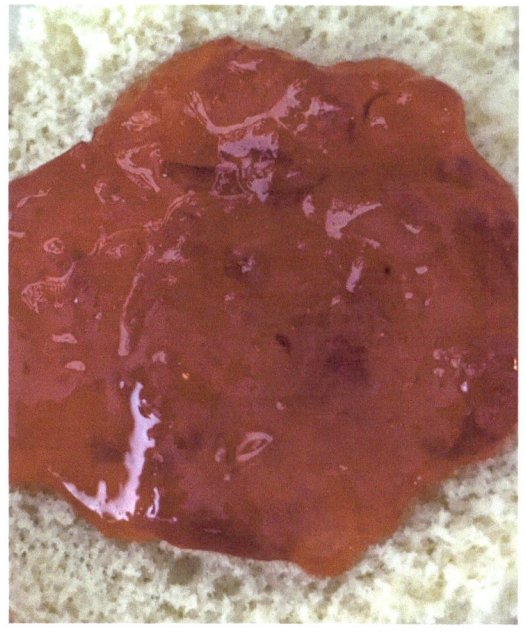

COOKING INSTRUCTIONS

» Lightly crush the fruit in a bowl.
» Place crushed berries in a deep sauté pan
» Add water, lemon juice, orange juice, and vanilla extract to the pan
» Simmer for 15 minutes
» Pass berries through a fine strainer to remove seeds
» Place the remaining mixture in a stock pot
» Simmer until thickened to a honey-like consistency
» Pour in jars and cool off prior sealing jars and let cool
» Seal jars when cooled
» Serve when appropriate

GARLIC MUSTARD

INVASIVE SPECIES PROFILE

Geography. The garlic mustard plant is native to Europe, Asia, and Africa. It was introduced to the United States in the mid-1800s, specifically in 1868 in Long Island, New York for it qualities as an herb, its medicinal qualities, and as a control plant for erosion. Garlic mustard is currently considered invasive in nearly 20 U.S. states.

Description. The best way to identify a garlic mustard plant, especially a young one, is to break/crumple a leaf and smell it. If it has a strong garlic smell, it is likely garlic mustard. The leaves of immature plants are dark green and shaped like a kidney with scalloped teeth along the edges. As the plant ages and grows, the leaves become more triangular-shaped and have sharper teeth along the edges. Leaf stalks of mature plants are covered with tiny hairs. The flowers of the garlic mustard are white, with four petals, four sepals, and six stamens. It spreads its seeds in the wind and emerges in fields and forests earlier than many native plants.

Threat. In spring, when native species are ready to grow, garlic mustard has blocked sunlight and out-competed them for moisture and vital nutrients. This invasive species that crowds out forest ecosystems also inhibits trees from growing.

GARLIC MUSTARD PASTA
SERVES 4

INGREDIENTS

8 oz	Garlic mustard stems, leaves, and/or flowers
2 oz	Garlic, minced
4 oz	Olive oil
¼ cup	Basil, fresh
4 oz	Parmesan cheese, grated
2 qt	Water
For 4	Spaghetti OR PASTA OF CHOICE
To Taste	Seasoning to taste

INVASIVE SPECIES RECIPE

COOKING INSTRUCTIONS

- Boil and drain spaghetti (pasta)
- Wash garlic mustard parts thoroughly under cool running water
- In a stock pot, bring 2 quarts of water to a boil
- Gently boil garlic mustard parts for 1 minute, remove from heat and drain
- Cool garlic mustard parts in iced water for 3-4 minutes
- Drain cooked, cold garlic mustard parts on a dry paper towel
- In a food processor, finely chop garlic, basil, and garlic mustard parts
- In a bowl, mix texture with olive oil and Parmesan cheese, seasoning to taste
- Stir into hot, cooked spaghetti of pasta of choice
- Serve hot with your favorite bread

WINTERCRESS

INVASIVE SPECIES PROFILE

Geography. Wintercress is native to western North America, North Africa, New Zealand, Eurasia, and parts of Europe. It is currently invasive in several U.S. states.

Description. Wintercress, also known as the yellow rocket, bittercress, and winter rocket is an herbaceous biennial plant in the mustard family.

Wintercress has stiff, branching stems that can grow several feet high. The leaves are relatively small and primarily oval, with rounded lobes near the end. It blooms as a spike of bright yellow flowers clustered at the ends of the stems.

It is also edible by humans and is a common food source for many wildlife. Many say that wintercress tastes similar to broccoli when it is properly cooked.

Threat. Wintercress reproduces quickly and in large quantities. It can rapidly take over space in any habitat in which it grows.

It out-competes native species for space and thereby affects native wildlife and insects in turn having an overall negative impact on the invaded ecosystem.

In addition, wintercress attracts leaf beetles in large quantities which also negatively impacts native plants.

Despite its edibility, wintercress is difficult to control in non-native ecosystems.

CREAMY WINTERCRESS DIP
SERVES 4

INGREDIENTS

4 cups	Wintercress leaves washed
¼ cup	Heavy cream
4 oz	Butter, unsalted
½ cup	Parmesan cheese,
½ cup	Grated Cheddar cheese, shredded
For 4	Toast, crackers of tortillas for dipping
To Taste	Seasoning to taste

COOKING INSTRUCTIONS

» In a sauté skillet, heat butter on medium heat until light brown
» Add wintercress leaves
» Stir until the leaves are fully cooked
» Add heavy cream and stir well
» Simmer for 5 minutes
» Add Parmesan and Cheddar
» Stir for 3 minutes
» Season to taste
» Remove from the heat
» Serve with toast, crackers, or tortillas

INVASIVE SPECIES RECIPE

PURSLANE

INVASIVE SPECIES PROFILE

Geography. The purslane plant is believed to be native to North Africa and was brought to America in the late 1600s for ornamental purposes.

Description. Purslane is an aggressive, annual succulent that forms a dense mat wherever it grows. Its stems are purple-red and radiate from a central point like spokes on a wheel. The oval, smooth, shiny, and succulent leaves are mostly arranged opposite along the stem. Purslane blooms small, single, five-petal flowers that can be of various colors and only open in the sunshine. Seeds are in small pods that are tiny and oval and range in color from reddish brown to black.

Though it is often considered a weed and grows across the country, it is not only edible but also full of nutrients, vitamins, and minerals. Purslane can help improve digestion, strengthen your immune system, and promote heart health. It is also a topical remedy for irritated skin and in wound care.

Threat. Due to prolific seed production and its ability to spread quickly, Purslane can rapidly colonize any site. It easily out-competes native species for space as well as nutrients. It creates thick mats of vegetation that blocks sunlight from reaching the soil.

Though it is often used in flowerbeds, it is considered a pest or invasive in all 50 states when it is not properly maintained and controlled.

PURSLANE
SERVES 4

INGREDIENTS

2 cups	Purslane leaves and stems
2 ea	Roma tomatoes, diced
4 oz	Feta cheese
4 tbsp	Olive oil
2 tbsp	Dijon mustard
2 tbsp	Balsamic vinegar
To Taste	Seasoning to taste

COOKING INSTRUCTIONS

- In a salad bowl, mix Dijon mustard with Balsamic vinegar
- Add olive oil and mix well.
- Add diced tomatoes and purslane into a salad bowl with dressing and mix well
- Season to taste mix and mix well
- Top with Feta cheese crumbles
- Serve fresh

JAPANESE KNOTWEED

INVASIVE SPECIES PROFILE

Geography. The Japanese knotweed plant is native to Asian countries, primarily Japan, China, Korea, and Taiwan. It is known as the most invasive plant in the entire world and is considered invasive in over 40 U.S. states.

Description. Japanese knotweed is often mistaken for bamboo since it has bamboo-like green stems that are hollow and segmented. Green heart-shaped leaves grow along the stem in a zigzag pattern. The stems and the leaves have purple speckles, and the plant blooms creamy white colored flowers in early Autumn.

Threat. Japanese knotweed is an aggressive species that pushes out native plant species with its dense colonies that take space and create shade that make areas no longer appropriate for native plants. It also has a negative impact on native wildlife who depend on native plants for food.

When Japanese knotweed is growing along rivers, ponds, and other waterways, it has been known to cause erosion and create problems with sedimentation at the water's edge.

Knotweed has also been known to negatively impact pipes, infrastructure, and residential and commercial building foundations.

Eradication of Japanese knotweed is difficult and costly. The city of New York, in 2010, spent over $1 million on eradication efforts for a 30 acre patch of knotweed.

KNOTWEED GARLIC BUTTER
SERVES 4

INGREDIENTS

2 lbs	Young shoots of knotweed peeled and cut into one inch pieces
4 oz	Butter, unsalted
1 oz	Sweet elephant garlic, chopped
1 tbsp	Brown sugar
1 oz	Lemon juice
2 oz	Orange juice
To Taste	Seasoning to taste

COOKING INSTRUCTIONS

- In a sauté skillet, heat butter until light brown
- Add knotweed shoots and sauté for 2 to 3 minutes on medium-high heat
- Add brown sugar and mix well
- Add lemon and orange juice to the skillet
- Sauté for 1 minute or until tender
- Season to taste
- Serve with favorite entrees or side dishes

STRAWBERRY GUAVA

INVASIVE SPECIES PROFILE

Geography. The strawberry guava, sometimes called a Cherry Guava, is native to South America, specifically Brazil. It was introduced in Hawaii and Florida in the 1800s and had dispersed into the wild by the 1950s. It is considered invasive in Hawaii, Florida, and Puerto Rico.

Description. The strawberry guava can grow as either a shrub or a tree, but a tree is the most common. Strawberry guava trees can grow up to 20 feet tall and have smooth bark. Their dark green leaves are several inches long, oblong in shape, and very aromatic.

They blossom one-inch white flowers with 4 - 5 petals and many stamens. After pollinating, they bear a red to purple fruit about the size of a golf ball.

Threat. The strawberry guava is an aggressive grower that forms shade-casting thickets, shading and crowding out native plants.

The leaves produce toxic chemicals that can prevent the growth of other plant species. It is considered one of the worst plant pests in Hawaii and is often found in sites disturbed by invasive feral pigs.

In Florida, the strawberry guava is a host plant for the Caribbean fruit fly that threatens citrus crops.

When uncontrolled the strawberry guava is a significant threat to the biodiversity of invaded areas.

STRAWBERRY GUAVA TOAST
SERVES 4

INGREDIENTS

1 cup	Strawberry guava fruit
½ cup	Sugar
¼ cup	Water
¼ cup	Orange juice
2 tbsp	Lemon juice
1 tbsp	Vanilla extract
Per Serving	Several slices of grilled toast

INVASIVE SPECIES RECIPE

COOKING INSTRUCTIONS

» Wash the strawberry guava well
» Trimmed off both ends of the guava
» Place in a food processor for 1 minute or until finely pureed
» Put the mixture into a saucepan with the sugar, water, orange juice, lemon juice, and vanilla extract
» Simmer over medium heat until thick coating consistency.
» Strain mixture if desired
» Let cool
» Serve over toast
» Perfect for breakfast

DANDELION

INVASIVE SPECIES PROFILE

Geography. The dandelion is native to most of Eurasia. It was brought to America in the mid-1600s by European settlers for uses as food and medicine. They primarily spread through windborne seeds and other natural disbursement methods.

The invasive dandelion is perhaps the nation's most persistent and widespread weed—appearing in all 50 states.

Description. The dandelion is a perennial, herbaceous plant that forms green rosettes of leaves with yellow flower clusters that rise from the center directly from the top of the root. The flowers develop into seed heads that are the fuzzy, fluffy white balls called pappus, with which everyone is familiar and has likely, at least once, blown into the wind on a blustery day.

Threat. Dandelions create dense circular mats of leaves that crowd out native species and reduce the vigor of the native species that survive.

Dandelion root systems are quite extensive and spread several meters in all directions. These roots sometimes strangle native species or minimize their growth potential.

An uncontrolled patch of invasive dandelion can have a huge negative impact on the biodiversity of the ecosystems where it is invasive.

DANDELION BACON VINAIGRETTE SALAD
SERVES 4

INGREDIENTS

8 oz	Dandelion stems
4 ea	Strips of bacon
1 tbsp	Dijon mustard
½ tbsp	Red wine vinegar
3 tbsp	Olive oil
1 tbsp	Garlic, minced
2 tbsp	Shallots, minced
To Taste	Seasoning to taste

COOKING INSTRUCTIONS

» Cut young green stems in half long-way and leave cut or torn into salad-size pieces
» In a sauté pan, cook bacon on medium-high heat until bacon is crisp
» Remove cooked bacon and pat dry on a paper towel
» Crumble bacon into bite-sized pieces.
» Keep the drippings from the bacon for the finish on the salad
» In a bowl, mix Dijon mustard, red wine vinegar, olive oil, shallots, garlic, and seasoning to taste and mix well
» Toss in dandelion and bacon pieces, then mix gently
» Pour hot bacon dripping over salad to taste and serve

EUROPEAN WATER CHESTNUT

INVASIVE SPECIES PROFILE

Geography. The European water chestnut is native to Europe, Asia, and Africa. It was brought to the United States by water gardeners, then inadvertently released into the waters of the Northeast, and it is spreading throughout New England and the Mid-Atlantic States, at least a dozen states overall.

Description. The water chestnut is a floating, rooted, aquatic, annual plant whose roots and stems are submerged and anchored in the substrate. The leaves are arranged in a floating rosette and are a darker green. They bloom perfect, single, small, white flowers with four petals in the center of the floating rosette. The plant's fruit is a sizable nut-like drupe with four sharp spines. It reproduces rapidly, producing up to 15 nuts, each containing a single seed per season.

Threat. The European water chestnut out-competes native species of aquatic vegetation for space in invaded waters. It can deplete oxygen from aquatic systems and reduce sunlight which is needed by native flora and fauna including fish, crustaceans, and other aquatic species.

They also create dense beds that are known to reduce water quality, often to the point of creating hypoxic conditions.

The water chestnut also clogs boat motors and can interfere with recreational and commercial fishing.

CANDIED EUROPEAN WATER CHESTNUTS
SERVES 4

INGREDIENTS

20 ea	European chestnuts peeled and washed
2 qt	Water
½ cup	Regular cane sugar
2 tbsp	Vanilla extract
1 ea	Whole lemon, squeezed for juice
2 ea	Whole oranges squeezed for juice
4 oz	Butter, unsalted
8 oz	Brown sugar cinnamon to taste
As needed	Cooking oil spray

INVASIVE SPECIES RECIPE

COOKING INSTRUCTIONS

- Add water, vanilla extract, cane sugar, freshly squeezed lemon juice, fresh squeezed orange juice, and water chestnuts to a large pot
- Simmer for 25 minutes or until water chestnuts are tender
- Remove chestnuts from the water and dry them on a paper towel
- In a hot skillet, melt butter until golden brown
- Add cinnamon and brown sugar, stir well
- Add dried water chestnut into a hot butter mixture
- Flip them regularly until coated with the caramelized mixture.
- Lightly spray oil evenly on a cookie tray
- Place caramelized water chestnuts onto a tray
- Let cool before serving

NOTES

BONUS INVASIVE SPECIES RECIPES
CAN'T BEAT 'EM, EAT 'EM INVASALAYA AND CAN'T BEAT 'EM, EAT 'EM GUMBO

CAN'T BEAT 'EM, EAT 'EM INVASALAYA™

Bonus Recipe — Chef Philippe Parola
Can't Beat 'Em, Eat 'Em

SERVES 8 - 10

INGREDIENTS

4 lbs	Nutria hind quarters*
4 lbs	Wild boar backstrap*
6 ea	Snow or Canada goose breasts*
2 cups	Long-grained white rice
2 cups	Chicken broth
2 cups	Beef broth
½ cup	Vegetable oil
2 ea	Onion, medium, diced
2 ea	Celery ribs, diced
1 cup	Green bell pepper, diced
6 ea	Garlic cloves, minced
4 ea	Whole bay leaves
To Taste	Seasoning to taste

* YOU CAN SUBSTITUTE ANY INVASIVE SPECIES MEAT!

COOKING INSTRUCTIONS

» Season all meat to taste
» Cook meat on a BBQ pit on medium-high until fully cooked
» Remove bones from cooked meat
» Dice meat into ½ inch cubes and set aside
» In a large cast-iron skillet, heat vegetable oil over medium-high heat
» Add onion, celery, and bell pepper
» Stir until golden brown
» Add garlic
» Stir well
» Add uncooked rice
» Stir well for 2 minutes
» Add bay leaves and all diced meat
» Stir well for 1 minute
» Add chicken broth and beef broth
» Stir well
» Simmer for 20 minutes
» Season to taste
» Serve hot

CAN'T BEAT 'EM, EAT 'EM GUMBO

BONUS RECIPE
Chef Philippe Parola
Can't Beat 'Em, Eat 'Em

SERVES 8 - 10

INGREDIENTS

2 ea	Nutria hind quarters*
2 lbs	Wild boar backstrap*
4 lbs	Copi (Invasive carp) boneless
2 cups	Onion, chopped
2 tbsp	Garlic, chopped
1 cup	Celery, diced
2 ea	Whole bay leaves
1 cup	Okra, sliced
2 qt	Beef broth
2 qt	Chicken broth
2 cup	Tomatoes, diced
¼ cup	Vegetable oil
¼ cup	Flour, regular
To Taste	Seasoning to taste

* YOU CAN SUBSTITUTE ANY INVASIVE SPECIES MEAT!

COOKING INSTRUCTIONS

» Season all meat to taste then grill for 30 minutes or fully cooked; remove bones from cooked meat and cut into bite-size pieces
» MAKE A ROUX (OR USE PRE-MADE GUMBO MIX)
  » Heat vegetable oil in a skillet on medium heat then add flour
  » STIR CONSTANTLY until the mixture is a rich brown color, being careful not to burn then remove from heat and set aside
» Add onions, garlic, and celery to hot roux (or gumbo mix) in the stock pot
» Stir well for 3 minutes
» Add tomato and okra
» Stir well then add chicken broth and beef broth
» Stir well
» Bring to a boil
» Add bay leaves
» Simmer for 15 minutes
» Add diced meat into pot
» Simmer for 15 minutes
» Add seasoned fish to the pot
» Gently stir until fully cooked
» Season to taste
» Serve with steamed rice

NOTES

SUPPORTIVE STATEMENTS AND LETTERS FROM EXPERTS

WHAT THE EXPERTS SAY

Mississippi Wildlife, Fisheries, and Parks

"Objective 4 of the Mississippi State Management Plan of Aquatic Invasive Species (2013) calls for state agencies to "control the spread of established invasive species through cooperative management activities designed to minimize impacts when eradication is not possible". In accordance with that plan, the MDWFP is ready to assist any firm with efforts to harvest these species and market products made for them. We thank you for your efforts and support with this matter."

Dennis Riecke
Fisheries Coordinator

Louisiana Wildlife and Fisheries

"Your recent inquiries and concern for Louisiana's coastal fisheries is also well warranted and very much appreciated. Louisiana's coastal waterways are thoroughly connected within basins influenced by rivers already infested with these destructive invasive species. Estimate indicate there are up 5.5 tons of Asian carp per river mile within the Mississippi River. Biologists in Louisiana predict there is no chance to effectively eradicate the species. Increased commercial harvest through effective marketing is currently the only option to help control the abundance and continued spread of Asian carp in Louisiana."

Tim Ruth
Fisheries Habitat Biologist DCL-A

Louisiana Wildlife and Fisheries

"Invasive Asian carp are established in Louisiana and there is little to no possibility for eradication. Building a market for Silverfin aka Asian carp is important both ecologically economically. Your efforts to bring this opportunity to Louisiana and the forefront of resource management are to be applauded. Please accept our support and continue your innovative approach."

Jack Montoucet
Secretary

Louisiana State University
Ag Center & Louisiana Sea Grant

"As a State/Federal program that promotes research, education, and outreach on coastal and marine issues, we are keenly aware of both the harmful impacts of these invasive species and the need to adequately address their spread in Louisiana's rivers and streams. We are also sensitive, in these difficult economic times, to the growing number of unemployed Louisianans and support any efforts to generate new businesses and new jobs. We are confident that your efforts will aid in remedying both of these issues not just in Louisiana, but in communities in all states of the Mississippi River Valley."

Dr. Julie A. Lively
Associate Professor & Fisheries Specialist

WHAT THE EXPERTS SAY

Arkansas Game and Fish Commission

"I would like to congratulate you on placing third in the recent Louisiana Seafood Cook-off, held during Navy week this year. Your use of invasive Silver Carp as the main item in your submission, is a statement to the potential these fish have as an accepted and sought-after item on the menus of our country's restaurants and other food market venues. On behalf of the Arkansas Game and Fish commission, I support your efforts and encourage you to continue the charge of developing interest in the consumption of invasive species."

Ben Batten
Deputy Director

Illinois Department of Natural Resources

"A brief note to commend you on years of determined work in considering the use of Bighead and Silver Carp in your Silverfin venture. The State of Illinois knows too well the concern of having these invasive species in our waterways and this concern is echoed in the Management and Control Plan for Bighead, Black, Grass, and Silver Carps in the United States. Recognizing the need for responsible harvest and all measures to prevent spread to uninvited waters is paramount. Congratulations on your top 3 dishes and most recent success of serving Silver Carp at the Louisiana Seafood Cook-off during Navy Week this year. What an opportunity to show the culinary value of these fish to our most valued citizens. Keep it going!"

Kevin Iron
Assistant Chief of Fisheries

Mississippi Department of Marine Resources

"We support your efforts to reduce the harmful effects of these exotic fish through your "Silverfin" campaign of harvesting and marketing for human consumption. Of all the Asian carp species, Silver Carp in particular seem to pose the greatest environmental threat. Their planktivorous feeding habits have the potential to harm estuarine ecosystems and the fisheries which are dependent on them. In addition, their large size and jumping behavior have caused significant injuries to boaters in infested areas."

Joseph D. Jewell
Director, Office of Marine Fisheries

Gulf and South Atlantic Regional Panel

"Your level of dedication to solving this national problem [Asian carp crisis] and the amount of work and research you and your group have dedicated to this project should be commended and really shows in the quality and thoroughness of your presentation. I know that your time is very valuable and we appreciate the effort you made to present this important project. Thanks again for the time to speak to us."

James R. Ballard
Sport Fish Restoration,
Aquatic Invasive Coordinator

A LETTER FROM CHEF MICHAEL JOHNSON

To my friend and mentor Chef Philippe Parola,

As a professional Chef that practices sustainability with such passion that I consider it a way of life, I am also a man obsessed with fishing and hunting. I spend a lot of time on the water and in the woods, furthering my understanding of both flora and fauna.

However, above all other things I am a father. A man who shoulders the responsibility of teaching his children how to make good decisions because from the day they are born a clock starts counting down to some obscure moment when they decide they're ready to do it for themselves. So, focusing on the quality time teaching them about the things I believe are the important.—character, Integrity, humility, and patience. But also, for me, that list must include sustainability; preserving our ecosystem for the generations to come.

Invasive species wreak havoc on our natural biosystems causing widespread loss of habitat and interrupting the natural chain of life. While some believe they can have a positive impact by filtering toxins or providing food source to a few select native species, the reality is that they threaten multitudes of additional native species which are highly reliant upon the natural resources which they are limited to within their geographical range. They carry great economic costs and even human health concerns with them. it's estimated that in the US alone we lose 150 billion a year in wasteful control methods and environmental loss.

So, in my mind I struggle with the idea of why we are trying to invent new expensive solutions for a problem that has an obvious and economical solution. We eat them. We pay the layfolk of the world, the fisherman, the farmers, and the hunters a competitive wage to trap and catch them. We bring them to market and create a demand for them by educating our youth who are, by and large, the most impressionable and open- minded about the subject. And, we tell the story about how to manage the invasive species numbers as well as how to prevent further impact from future happenings.

We encourage chefs to serve them and educate diners to the viability of the food source. Lastly, we support those who are carrying the torch in trying to make a difference in our communities in trying to preserve our natural resources.

Chef Michael Johnson
Executive Chef
LSU Athletics

SUPPORT FROM LOUISIANA SEAFOOD EXCHANGE

An Open Letter from Robert Walker; Owner/General Manager of Louisiana Seafood Exchange, Inc.

Tuesday, September 3, 2013

As an owner of the largest multi-varietal seafood processor/wholesaler/distributor in the Gulf coast area, I believe there is a strong need for another source of indigenous seafood like the Asian carp aka Silverfin™, for not only here in Louisiana but the nation as well. Our company, like many others in this industry, is constantly searching for quality seafood products that are in demand, have great flavor profiles, economical, abundant, and safe. My experience with Chef Philippe Parola and his Silverfin fish product allows me to state this fish meets those requirements. And with a customer base of over 500 restaurants, supermarkets, and institutional foodservice outlets here on the Gulf coast, allows the comfort of knowing there are more options for them.

Our local industry's access to our own abundant natural resources of seafood has been drastically reduced and limited by over regulation. This trend has played out all over the country in the last two decades causing shortages here on domestically produced seafood and an over reliance on massive importation of foreign seafood. Aside from the instability associated with importing products from foreign countries, we face the possibility of hidden health risks that may also be associated with imported seafood products.

The abundance of Asian carp here in the U.S. is ripe for creating a high quality, fairly inexpensive, end product that can be marketed nationwide to consumers through the retail, foodservice, and institutional business sectors. There is a definitive need for these types of fish products.

I can see a very useful purpose for expanding the creation and availability of the carp products. I also believe that my company would be very active in helping to cultivate the demand of this product and will commit to marketing these products.

It is also my opinion that the time for embracing a fishery and a production method for those fish is long overdue. This fishery and production thereof will be supported by our leaders and is embraced by the national and local media; instrumental in successfully unveiling and profiting from such an endeavor. It is now time to move to the production and marketing side of this fish story.

Thanks,

Robert "Robbie" Walker
Owner,
Louisiana Seafood Exchange, Inc.
11975 Lakeland Park Blvd.
Baton Rouge, Louisiana 70809
225-756-5225
www.louisianaseafoodexchange.net

Chef Philippe gives a special thank you to Robbie Walker at Louisiana Seafood Exchange for his continuing support of his invasive species efforts.

SUPPORT FROM TIM RUTH AT LOUISIANA WILDLIFE AND FISHERIES

From: Tim Ruth <truth@wlf.la.gov>
Date: Wed, Feb 12, 2020, 4:04 PM
Subject: Asian Carp in Coastal Louisiana
To: Philippe Parola <chef@chefphilippe.com>

Dear Chef Philippe,

Please consider this letter of support for your continued efforts to provide a solution to the increasing invasion of Asian carp in Louisiana. Your recent inquiries and concern for Louisiana's coastal fisheries is also well warranted and very much appreciated. Louisiana's coastal waterways are thoroughly connected within basins influenced by rivers already infested with these destructive invasive species. Estimates indicate there are up to 5.5 tons of Asian carp per mile within the Mississippi River. Biologists in Louisiana predict there is no chance to effectively eradicate the species. Increased commercial harvest through effective marketing is currently the only option to help control the abundance and continued spread of Asian carp in Louisiana.

The four species of Asian carp invading Louisiana's estuaries (Silver, Bighead, Grass and Black carp) are highly prolific, destructive to our aquatic ecosystems and threatening our coastal economy. Silver carp can tolerate up to 12ppt salinity and low dissolved oxygen. They consume phytoplankton and zooplankton and can live up to 20 years. Bighead and Silver carp can consume up to 50% of their body weight daily and grow to exceed 80lb pounds. This far exceeds the consumption rate and growth potential of native estuarine planktivores like shad, herring and menhaden. The reproduction rate of the invasive carps also exceeds the rate of many native estuarine species. A mature female can spawn up to 5 million eggs a year. LDWF has documented reproduction in Louisiana as far south as the Atchafalaya River Delta. Further upstream spawning may be occurring up to 4 times a year. Another injurious member of the Asian carps, Grass carp can consume up to 40% of their body weight in submerged aquatic vegetation (SAV) per day. SAV in our estuaries is of extreme importance to the ecosystem. It is one of the most critical components of the estuarine food web. SAV provides food and nursery areas for larval and juvenile aquatic species as well as food for native and migratory waterfowl.

In 2019 the Mississippi River in Louisiana reached record levels and remained above flood stage for a historic length of time. The Bonnet Carre Spillway operated for a record 123 days and flooding within the Atchafalaya Basin persisted through August. Furthermore, there has been an increased frequency in flood events requiring the operation of the Spillway. Five of the 13 total spillway operation events have occurred since 2008 and its operation has been required 3 of the past 4 years. The Louisiana Department of Wildlife and Fisheries is currently conducting biological sampling and analysis of commercial and recreational species along the coast. Results released in September 2019 indicate a notable reduction in the availability of important species.

As you are aware, recreational fishing in Coastal Louisiana provides a significant economic benefit to our state. LDWF estimates indicate the total economic impact of saltwater recreational fishing in Louisiana at $757,091,876, supporting 7,753 jobs and generating $49,976,489 in state and local tax revenues. Increased freshwater introduction associated with recent floods produce several environmental factors which can reduce the abundance of marine and estuarine species. However, the effects of increased biomass introduction of Asian carp and further distribution of the 4 invasive species is unknown. During the peak of this year's flood Asian carp were found over 100 miles west of the mouth of the Atchafalaya River and over 30 miles east of the Mississippi River in Mississippi Sound. Biologists consider the recent expansion of Asian carp along our coast directly related to lower salinities produced by high river levels. Biologists also predict salinities will return to normal and Asian carp will retreat to areas of lower salinities in the upper part of our estuaries. Researchers with USACE and USGS are currently working on salinity tolerance studies for the species.

From: Tim Ruth <truth@wlf.la.gov>
Date: Wed, Feb 12, 2020, 4:04 PM
Subject: Asian Carp in Coastal Louisiana
To: Philippe Parola <chef@chefphilippe.com>

LDWF biologists and invasive species researchers still have many unanswered questions in regards to the specific threats of Asian carp to Louisiana's coastal fisheries. Recent facts indicate an increasing abundance and worsening impacts. Asian carp population dynamics data are currently lacking for Louisiana's waterways. However, we can confidently state that increased commercial harvest of Asian carp in Louisiana will decrease the species biomass and promote proliferation of native species.

Please continue your Silverfin marketing efforts with urgency. It is currently the only viable management option to limit the negative effects to our ecosystem and valuable coastal fisheries in Louisiana.

Tim Ruth
Fisheries Habitat Biologist DCL-A
Office: (985) 882-0027   Mobile: (225) 571-3976

INDEX

A

Africa 36, 44, 58, 76, 110, 112, 114, 122
Alaine 8
Alla's Fine Art i 7
alligator 12, 13, 14, 21, 32
Alligator Gar 31
Almonds 47
Ambassador 5
American Bullfrog 1, 100
Apple Snail iv, 66, 67
arctic 88
Argentina 74
Ariana 8
Armenia 106
Armored Catfish in Wine and Capers iii, 43
Armored Sailfin Catfish iii, 42
Asia 17, 34, 36, 38, 40, 44, 48, 52, 60, 62, 80, 96, 108, 110, 122
Aurbin Dickey 7
Australia 40, 50, 76
Autumn 1, 108, 109, 116
Autumn Olive/Berry 1, 108
Autumn Olive Jelly 1, 109
Avocados 53, 95
Axis (Spotted) Dear iv, 78
Azov Sea 64

B

bacon 121
baking 35, 39, 41, 45, 49, 59, 81, 85, 91
Balsamic 115
Baltas 7
Bananas 107
basil 45, 111
Baton Rouge ii, 7
bay leaves 75, 126, 127
Beast Feast 31
Beef broth 71, 99, 126, 127
bell peppers 63
Berry iv, 1, 71, 108
Beth Townsend i, 7
Bighead Carp aka Copi iii, 52
Billy Frioux 16
Bisque iv, 59
blackberries 71
Blackberry 1, 71, 106, 107
Black Carp iii, 38, 39
Black Sea 64
Black tiger shrimp 60, 61
Black Tiger Shrimp iv, 60
Boar iv, 10, 13, 70, 71
Bolivia 74
bones 28, 35, 49, 53, 81, 126, 127
Bonus 1, 126, 127

Brandy 59
Brazil 74, 94, 118
breadcrumbs 35, 65, 67, 97
Breadcrumbs 35, 65, 91, 97
Brown sugar 51, 79, 117, 123
Brown Trout iii, 36, 37
Brown Trout Pecan iii, 37
Bullfrog 1, 100, 101
Bullfrog Legs 1, 101
Burgers 1, 97
Butter 1, 35, 37, 41, 47, 59, 61, 65, 67, 71, 79, 81, 85, 101, 107, 113, 117, 123

C

cabbage 75
Cajun iii, iv, 4, 9, 23, 24, 39, 57
Cajun Style Copi (Black Carp) iii, 39
Cambodia 50
Canada iv, 90, 91, 100, 126
Canada Goose iv, 90, 91
Candied European Water Chestnuts 1, 123
Cane sugar 73
Capers iii, 43
carp 11, 13, 16, 17, 18, 19, 20, 22, 23, 24, 25, 27, 28, 29, 30, 31, 32, 34, 35, 38, 39, 48, 49, 52, 53, 127, 130, 131
Carrots 51, 63, 75
Cartoon 136
Caspian Sea 64
Celery 35, 63, 99, 126, 127
Central America 84, 94
Cheddar 49, 113
cheese 39, 49, 65, 67, 91, 95, 105, 111, 113, 115
Chef Philippe Parola i, ii, iii, 2, 3, 8, 10, 17, 22, 25, 27, 29, 132
Cherry iv, 79, 118
Cherry preserves 79
Chestnuts 1, 123
Chicken stock 63, 67, 77, 87
China 3, 34, 38, 46, 48, 50, 52, 96, 104, 116
Chowder iv, 63
Cilantro 37, 41, 47, 97
Clam iv, 62, 63
clam juice 63
Cody Sibley i, 7
Copi iii, iv, 16, 18, 19, 25, 34, 35, 38, 39, 48, 49, 52, 53, 127
Copi (Bighead Carp) Sliders iv, 53
Copi (Grass Carp) Au Gratin iii, 49
Copi (Silver Carp) Fish Cakes iii, 35
Cordon Bleu 3, 4
corn 57, 101
Corn meal 95
Corwin 4, 16, 31
COVID-19 17
crawfish 24

INDEX

crayfish 38, 56
Creamy Wintercress Dip 113
Crock Pot 75
Cuvee 4

D

Dandelion 1, 120, 121
Dandelion Bacon Vinaigrette Salad 1, 121
Danielle 8
daughters 6
David Roshto 6
Dawn Aubrey 25
Deer iv, 78, 79
Dijon iv, 81, 115, 121
Dill 73
dipping sauce 35
Duck iv, 84, 85

E

Ecuador 94
egg 35, 97, 101, 105
Eric Bucker 28
Europe 12, 36, 58, 76, 86, 110, 112, 122
European Green Crab iv, 58
European Rabbit iv, 76, 77
European Rabbit with Mushrooms iv, 77
Evelyn Sanguinetti 27
Ewell Smith, 27, 32
Experts 1, 44, 129, 130

F

Family 6
Feral Goat iv, 80, 81
Feral Goat Dijon iv, 81
feral hogs 70
feral pigs 70, 118
Feral Swine iv, 70
Feral Swine (Wild Boar) iv, 70
fillets 35, 37, 39, 41, 43, 45, 47, 53
FISH CAKES 35
Flambé 1, 107
Florida Keys 94
Flour 43, 71, 87, 99, 127
Foodex 5
Fox Squirrel iv, 72, 73
Fox Squirrel Ravigote iv, 73
France 3, 4, 6, 22
Fred Townsend i, 7
French Polynesia 40
Fried Bullfrog Legs 1, 101
Fried Green Iguana Tacos iv, 95

G

Garlic 1, 23, 39, 41, 47, 57, 63, 65, 67, 71, 75, 77, 89, 91, 97, 99, 101, 110, 111, 117, 121, 126, 127
Garlic Butter 1, 117
Garlic Mustard 1, 110, 111
Garlic Mustard Pasta 111
Gen-Z 26
George H. W. Bush 3
Gerald R. Ford 3
GNU Free Documentation License 20, 36
Goat iv, 80, 81
Golden Clam iv, 62, 63
Golden Clam Chowder iv, 63
Gourmet Python Burgers 1, 97
Grass Carp iii, 48, 49
Grass Carp aka Copi iii, 48
Green beans 51
green crab 58
Green Crab Bisque iv, 59
Green Iguana iv, 94, 95
Green onions, 51, 85
Guava 1, 118, 119
Gulf of Mexico. 40, 44
Gulf Seafood Foundation 27
gumbo 15, 125, 127
Gumbo 1, 126
GUMBO 127

H

Half & Half 91
Ham 105
Heart Healthy 75
Heavy cream 49, 61, 63, 77, 87, 105, 113
Helge Busch-Paulick 36
Himalayan 1, 71, 106, 107
Himalayan Blackberry Flambé 1, 107
hindquarters 73
Hong Kong 50
Hugo Sdralek 31

I

ice cream 107
Iceland 36
Iguana iv, 94, 95
Illinois iii, 11, 16, 18, 25, 27, 28, 29, 38, 131
India 50, 78, 96, 104
Indonesia 50
INVASALAYA™ 1, 126
invasive 5, 6, 7, 8, 9, 10, 11, 13, 14, 16, 17, 18, 19, 20, 21, 22, 23, 24, 25, 27, 28, 29, 30, 31, 32, 36, 38, 40, 42, 44, 46, 48, 50, 52, 56, 58, 60, 62, 70, 72, 74, 76, 78, 80, 84, 86, 88, 90, 94, 96, 98, 100, 104, 108, 110, 112, 114, 116, 118, 120, 130, 131, 132

INDEX

J

Japan 3, 4, 5, 50, 104, 116
Jeff Corwin 16
Jelly 1, 109
Jeremy Wade 32
Jolie 8
Jumping Carp. 34

K

Kaltakdjian 7
Kevin Irons 25
Kit Smith 25
Knotweed 1, 116, 117
Knotweed Garlic Butter 1, 117
Kobrossi 7
Krisite F. Gauthreaux 7
Kudzu 1, 11, 104, 105
Kudzu Pie 1, 105
Kudzu Vine 1, 104

L

Laos 50
Lemon iv, 23, 37, 39, 41, 43, 47, 61, 63, 89, 101, 107, 109, 117, 119
Lemon Cream Sauce iv, 61
lettuce 53, 95
Lionfish iii, 40, 41
Lionfish Meunière iii, 41
Louisiana iii, 1, 3, 4, 5, 6, 7, 10, 12, 13, 14, 15, 16, 17, 18, 21, 22, 23, 24, 27, 28, 29, 31, 32, 38, 56, 57, 70, 84, 130, 131, 133, 134
low-sodium 75
LSU 30, 132

M

Malaysia 50
Marinara 45, 91
Mask-Off Publishing 7
Mayonnaise 35, 97
Mexico 40, 44, 66, 84, 94
Mike Johnson 30
Milk 101
Mississippi River Basin iii, 18, 20, 24, 56, 62
Mozzarella 91, 105
Muscovy iv, 84, 85
Muscovy Duck iv, 84, 85
Mushrooms iv, 57, 77, 91
Myanmar 50

N

Navy iii, 22, 23, 131
Navy Cook-Off Recipe 23
Nepal 78
New Orleans, 22, 32
NOLA iii, 22, 23
Northern Snakehead Fish iii, 46
Notes Sheet iv, 1, 54, 68, 82, 92, 102, 124, 128
Nutmeg 105
Nutria iii, iv, 13, 14, 15, 74, 75, 126, 127

O

ohn Bel Edwards, 32
Olive 1, 23, 41, 43, 45, 51, 61, 63, 81, 89, 91, 108, 109, 111, 115, 121
Olive oil 41, 43, 45, 51, 61, 63, 81, 89, 91, 111, 115, 121
omega-3 19
One Pot Glazed Snow Goose iv, 89
Onion 35, 63, 71, 75, 77, 89, 91, 99, 126, 127
Orange iv, 85, 89, 107, 109, 117, 119
Orange juice 85, 89, 107, 109, 117, 119

P

Paraguay 74
Parmesan 39, 49, 65, 67, 91, 105, 111, 113
pasta 45, 91, 111
patties 35, 97
Paul Prudhomme 18
Pecan iii, 37
Philippines 50
pickle 73
Pie 1, 105
Pigeon iv, 86, 87
plecos 42
Preheat 35, 39, 41, 45, 49, 59, 65, 79, 81, 85, 91, 105
Purpose Promotions; 7
purslane 114, 115
Python 1, 11, 96, 97

R

Rabbit iv, 76, 77
Ragondin iv, 14, 75
Ragondin (Nutria) Crock Pot (Heart Healthy) iv, 75
Ranch dressing 53
Red bell peppers 63
Red Crawfish iv, 56, 57
Red-Eared Slider Turtle 1, 98, 99
Red-Eared Slider Turtle Soup 1, 99
Red onion 45, 51, 53
Red wine vinegar 73, 89, 121
refrigerator 35, 97
Rice 39, 51
River Monsters 32
Rock Dove iv, 86, 87
Rock Dove (Pigeon) Stew iv, 87
Romaine 53
ROY BRABH 19

INDEX

rum 107
Russia 34, 38, 46, 52, 88
Rusty Kimbal 31

S

Salad 1, 115, 121
Salsa 95
Salt 57
sauté 37, 43, 47, 51, 53, 61, 67, 89, 91, 107, 109, 113, 117, 121
Seasoning 23, 35, 37, 41, 43, 47, 49, 51, 53, 59, 61, 63, 65, 67, 71, 73, 75, 77, 79, 81, 85, 87, 89, 91, 95, 97, 99, 101, 105, 111, 113, 115, 117, 121, 126, 127
Seattle Seahawks 30
Serop's 7
Shallots 65, 97, 121
Shrimp iv, 27, 60, 61
Shrimp in Lemon Cream Sauce iv, 61
silver carp 23, 34, 35
sister 6
Snail iv, 66, 67
snakehead 46, 47
Snakehead Fish Almondine iii, 47
Snow Goose iv, 88, 89
Soup 1, 99
Sour cream 35, 95
South America 66, 74, 84, 94, 118
Southern Baked Tilapia iii, 45
South Pacific 40
Soy sauce 51
Spaghetti 111
Spotted) Deer 78
Squirrel iv, 72, 73
Sri Lanka 78
Stew iv, 87
Strawberry 1, 118, 119
Strawberry Guava Toast 1, 119
Stuffed Zebra Mussel iv, 65
subarctic 88
sugar 23, 51, 73, 79, 85, 89, 107, 117, 119, 123
Swamp eel 51
Swamp Eel iii, 50, 51
Swamp Eel Stir Fry iii, 51
Swamp People 32
Sweet Berry Wild Boar iv, 71
Sweet & sour sauce 51
Sysco 28

T

Tacos iv, 95
Taco shells 95
Taiwan 3, 15, 50, 104, 116
Thailand 50
Tilapia iii, 19, 44, 45
Tim Creehan 4, 5
Toast 113
Tomato 59, 67, 73, 99
Tomatoes 39, 53, 95, 127
tomato sauce 45, 67
Tom Foley 5
tortillas 95
Triple Sec 107
Troy Landry 32
Tulane University 32
Turtle 1, 98, 99

U

unsalted 35, 37, 41, 47, 59, 61, 65, 67, 71, 79, 81, 85, 107, 113, 117, 123
Uruguay 74

V

Vegetable oil 59, 77, 87, 99, 126, 127
Vietnam 17
Vinaigrette 1, 121
vinegar 73, 89, 115, 121

W

Water 1, 34, 35, 51, 57, 59, 67, 97, 111, 119, 122, 123
Water Chestnuts 1, 123
White wine 37, 39, 41, 43, 51, 61, 63, 65
wine 23, 37, 39, 41, 43, 51, 59, 61, 63, 65, 71, 73, 77, 79, 81, 85, 87, 89, 99, 121
Wintercress 1, 112, 113
Wisconsin 24

Z

Zebra Mussel iv, 64, 65

INVASIVE SPECIES AND RECIPE QUICK REFERENCE

INVASIVE SPECIES PROFILES

American Bullfrog 100
Apple Snail 66
Armored Sailfin Catfish 42
Autumn Olive/Berry 108
Axis (Spotted Deer) 78
Bighead Carp aka Copi 52
Black Carp aka Copi 38
Black Tiger Shrimp 60
Brown Trout 36
Burmese Python 96
Canada Goose 90
Dandelion 120
European Green Crab 58
European Rabbit 76
European Water Chestnut 122
Feral Goat 80
Feral Swine (Wild Boar) 70
Fox Squirrel 72
Garlic Mustard 110
Golden Clam 62
Grass Carp aka Copi 48
Green Iguana 94
Himalayan Blackberry 106
Japanese Knotweed 116
Kudzu Vine 104
Lionfish 40
Muscovy Duck 84
Northern Snakehead Fish 46
Nutria 74
Purslane 114
Red Crawfish 56
Red-Eared Slider Turtle 98
Rock Dove (Common Pigeon) 86
Silver Carp aka Copi 34
Snow Goose 88
Strawberry Guava 118
Swamp Eel 50
Tilapia 44
Wintercress 112
Zebra Mussel 64

INVASIVE SPECIES RECIPES

Apple Snail Provençale 67
Armored Catfish in Wine and Capers 43
Autumn Olive Jelly 109
Axis Deer with Cherry Sauce 79
Brown Trout Pecan 37
Cajun Style Boiled Red Crawfish 57
Cajun Style Copi (Black Carp) 39
Can't Beat 'Em, Eat 'Em GUMBO 127
Can't Beat 'Em, Eat 'Em INVASALAYA™ 126
Canada Goose Parmigiana 91
Candied European Water Chestnuts 123
Copi (Bighead Carp) Sliders 53
Copi (Grass Carp) Au Gratin 49
Copi (Silver Carp) Fish Cakes 35
Creamy Wintercress Dip 113
Dandelion Bacon Vinaigrette Salad 121
European Rabbit with Mushrooms 77
Feral Goat Dijon 81
Fox Squirrel Ravigote 73
Fried Bullfrog Legs 101
Fried Green Iguana Tacos 95
Garlic Mustard Pasta 111
Golden Clam Chowder 63
Gourmet Python Burgers 97
Green Crab Bisque 59
Himalayan Blackberry Flambé 107
Knotweed Garlic Butter 117
Kudzu Pie 105
Lionfish Meunière 41
Muscovy Duck à L'Orange 85
One Pot Glazed Snow Goose 89
Purslane Salad 115
Ragondin (Nutria) Crock Pot (Heart Healthy) 75
Red-Eared Slider Turtle Soup 99
Rock Dove (Pigeon) Stew 87
Shrimp in Lemon Cream Sauce 61
Snakehead Fish Almondine 47
Southern Baked Tilapia 45
Strawberry Guava Toast 119
Stuffed Zebra Mussel 65
Swamp Eel Stir Fry 51
Sweet Berry Wild Boar 71

www.ingramcontent.com/pod-product-compliance
Lightning Source LLC
Chambersburg PA
CBHW041150060526
44107CB00141B/1122